Daughters on Duty

Daughters on Duty: A Caregiver's Guide to Managing Medical Matters
Copyright © 2024 by Jackie McDaniels

Published in the United States of America

Library of Congress Control Number: 2024905567
ISBN   Paperback: 979-8-89091-516-0
ISBN   eBook: 979-8-89091-517-7

All rights reserved. No part of this publication may be reproduced, stored in a retrieval system or transmitted in any way by any means, electronic, mechanical, photocopy, recording or otherwise without the prior permission of the author except as provided by USA copyright law.

The opinions expressed by the author are not necessarily those of ReadersMagnet, LLC.

ReadersMagnet, LLC
10620 Treena Street, Suite 230 | San Diego, California, 92131 USA
1.619. 354. 2643 | www.readersmagnet.com

Book design copyright © 2024 by ReadersMagnet, LLC. All rights reserved.

Cover design by Erika Obando
Interior design by Daniel Lopez

Daughters on Duty

A Caregiver's Guide to Managing Medical Matters

JACKIE McDANIELS

ReadersMagnet, LLC

CONTENTS

Dedication vii

Mom and Me: A Poem by Jackie McDaniels ix

Introduction...xi

Chapter One: The Call... 1

Chapter Two: An Emergency Room Visit 17

Chapter Three: Admission-what happens now? 39

Chapter Four: Discharge from the Hospital 57

Chapter Five: After the Hospital 72

Conclusion.. 93

Epilogue 99

Acknowledgements... 101

About the Author 105

Mom's Blue Ribbon Cake: A Poem by Jackie McDaniels 107

DEDICATION

Dedicated to Mom and Dad, for the gift of your love and the precious legacy of your life together.

MOM AND ME:
A Poem by Jackie McDaniels

When I was young she cared for me.
She taught me right from wrong to see.
I tried her patience, made her mad.
Broke her heart and made her sad.
Through it all she was always there.
She dried my tears, told me life's not fair.
Then I grew up and moved away.
Unaware our roles would switch some day.
She shouldn't drive, she can barely see.
Her hearing is bad. How can this be?
I do my best to make it right.
To help her live a happy life.
She cared for Grandma, in her time.
Now I see the role is mine.
Sometimes I feel my life's on hold.
Who will care for me when I get old?
The roles reverse, generations change.
We take our turn, we rearrange.
We love them so, our mothers dear.
How blessed we are to have them near.

INTRODUCTION

The day my mother-in-law was released from the hospital after having her first heart attack I was the one to pick her up and transfer her home. I showed up at the hospital, got all the doctor's orders, her list of medications (there were thirteen), and carefully got her ninety pound, ninety-year-old body into the car and back to her house. We were doing pretty well getting out of the car, and got to the entry stairs next to the flower bed okay, when before my widening eyes and before I could do anything about it she rolled off of my arm and into her beautiful ruby red rhododendron. Thankfully, the rhododendron suspended her frail frame two feet above the ground, at least long enough for me to pull her out. It was not such a great way for a somewhat new daughter-in-law-turned-caregiver to make her mother-in-law feel confident about what kind of care she might expect. I was mortified… clearly I was nowhere near "ready." I made a note, for future reference, to have a darn good grip on her at all times. In spite of our rocky start, I was involved in her care until she died, at ninety-four.

Do you see your Mom or Dad starting to slow down, seeming more forgetful than usual, or having reasons to see a doctor more often? Maybe you have a friend dealing with aging parents, and it's made you think about what's going to happen when your folks get to that point, the point when they ask for help. The reality is, they probably aren't going to actually tell you when they need help. They will just struggle through until there is some kind of crisis. If you're not sure if there is a plan for these things, or if an initial event has already occurred, you need to start really paying attention and asking some questions.

I wasn't really ready to step into the role when my mother-in-law and I had our first caregiving encounter. My husband and I had been married for only a couple of years. Our two sons from previous lives and relationships were lovingly raised and already living on their own. We had good jobs that we liked. (We worked at the same software company. I married my boss. Not a good idea in every situation, but we're thirty years into it now, and still going strong.) We went out to dinner every Friday night, and spent weekends in the summer and fall out in the woods, went snow skiing in the winter. Our time was our own. I even had a vanity license plate made for my husband for his fiftieth birthday that said, "KDSAGIN". The cruel truth was that it was our parents who got to become kids again, and we had to be the responsible ones to take care of them.

Sixty-five percent of seniors who need ongoing care rely on family or friends to help them and enable them to stay in their home for as long as possible. That doesn't mean as long as is practical, because most of the time the fear of losing their independence, the logistics of loved ones living hours away, or finances create a situation that leaves a senior in their home well beyond what is practical. The value of the care and services we provide, in dollars, is in the hundred billions and priceless by any other standard. The personal cost of that care (often unpaid in practice) on the caregiver can become overwhelming and exhausting. How many hats might you wear?

If you, like me, have found or are just finding yourself in the position to take on this role, you could call yourself a "Mad Hatter", at least part of the time. Some of those hats include hands-on nursing care, care management, surrogate decision-maker, advocate, daughter, friend, companion, housekeeper, grocery shopper, taxi cab driver, family information center, constant worrier, and the list goes on. I'm here to tell you that whatever you are doing to help your mom or dad, in-laws, aunts or uncles, friends or neighbors, you are a blessing to them. You are also a blessing to all the others who love them but don't have the time, patience or physical locality to take on these tasks. A friend of mine once told me that as caregivers, we were earning the jewels for our crown in heaven. Some of us are going to have a lot of bling!

This book is intended to help you and your senior navigate the often frightening, always stressful, temple of the medical machine the hospital via the emergency room. I want to share the knowledge I have absorbed while spending countless hours inside the machine, over the more than sixteen years since I first began caring for my husband's mother, and subsequently cared for my own mother. Navigating our complicated health care system is difficult at best, and especially frustrating if you don't know how it actually works. Having the information you need and a reality-based expectation of how the machine works will help you work productively with the system to get Mom the care she needs and deserves.

I don't want to ignore or discount the advances modern medicine has made, or the outcomes that allow us to live longer, more active lives than our ancestors but the system that provides these things is a mess. Knowing more about how emergency rooms, hospitals, rehabilitation/skilled nursing facilities and assisted living facilities operate will help you avoid a great deal of frustration and worry when a crisis occurs that puts Mom in the hospital for the first time or back again. A working knowledge of how the medical community functions will also help you to advocate for the best care your loved one can receive, and that is the bottom line.

This book is set up to guide you, step-by-step, through the whole journey from the time you get "the call" to let you know that Mom is having a crisis. (That call may be the first one to make you run out the door with your hair on fire.) In this book, I discuss the issues and considerations at each step of recovery from said crisis, and back to whatever living arrangement may be needed to keep Mom safe and receiving the appropriate care. Every crisis is different and every family is unique. This book doesn't have all the answers, but it has practical guidance you can use to *find* the answers that are right for you and your situation.

One other "survival technique" that has worked for me for years is to keep my sense of humor intact, and you must keep yours. There's a lot about being a caregiver that isn't fun or funny. A lot of the subject matter is plenty serious but don't be afraid to laugh at the things that are funny. It will lighten your mood, and relieve the sense of burden, on you well as those around you.

CHAPTER ONE: THE CALL

"It's not a terrible thing that we feel fear when faced with the unknown.
It is part of being alive, something we all share."
Pema Chodron

What started out as a beautiful August day in the year of the millennium turned into one of the worst days of my life and changed it forever, in some unexpected ways. My husband and I had been out all afternoon, and we returned home to find a phone message from my brother, Mitch. It was to be "the call" that would change my world, and place me on the path to becoming my mother's caregiver and advocate for over a decade.

I knew immediately something was terribly wrong. His message hadn't been more than, "Give me a call Sis. As soon as you can." When I returned the call and asked my brother how he was, his first answer was, "Not so good." He then went on to tell me that Dad was in the hospital. He explained that Dad had been out mowing the field on the back side of his one acre property, riding his John Deere mower. On his way back to the barn, he ran over some barbed wire, and it became tangled in the mower. My brother said Dad had disengaged the mower blade and put the machine in neutral, but that the engine was still running when he got behind it and started jerking on the wire to free it. Somehow, this popped the mower into reverse, and it knocked Dad over and rolled on top of him. He was trapped under the running lawn mower, while it sat smack on the middle of his body.

As much as he fought to get the monster off of him, Dad at seventy two, with his body weakened by Parkinson's, was no match for the six hundred pound John Deere. He had been trapped under the thing for nearly an hour and a half, before my brother found him. As soon as Mitch saw him, the shock prompted an infusion of adrenaline that gave him the strength to lift the lawn mower off of Dad. Mitch's wife then called 911, and Dad was rushed to the hospital in Pasco, WA.

Mitch said Dad had sustained second and third degree burns on his hands, arms, abdomen and groin. While we talked, Dad was still in emergency, where they were dressing his wounds. All of this was happening more than 150 miles away from where I stood, in my Post Falls, Idaho home. I couldn't get there fast enough.

The local community hospital near my parents' home did the best they could with the resources they had. Dad needed to have someone with him around the clock, to make sure he didn't hurt himself or mess with his dressings while in the fog of all the morphine they were pumping into him. My siblings and I took turns sitting with him, because the hospital didn't have staff to provide enough supervision. For the family, it was important to have one of us there just to make sure he was okay. After a couple of days, we had him moved to a bigger hospital in Spokane, WA for more advanced care.

Dad endured weeks of critical care and unimaginably painful, twice daily treatments for his burns. Mom was with him, at least as much as we would let her stay. She was seventy-one at the time, and had her own health challenges as an insulin dependent diabetic as well as visual impairment from macular degeneration. My siblings and I did our best to make sure she took care of herself while she watched over the love of her life in critical care. We had to push her out the door of his room to eat and sleep, neither of which she was very interested in doing during that time. She sat for hours and hours by his side, day after day, and it got to the point where nurses, doctors and family alike would enter the room and ask, "Hi Mary. Did you eat yet?" After a while it sounded more like, "D'jeet yet?" Strangely, that made-up word is still used in our family.

After going through an initial surgery to cover his wounds with cadaver skin, we thought he was making progress. Yet the extended time of immobility, pain medications and burn debridement treatments started taking a toll on the rest of his body, and he started to develop respiratory congestion. My mother, sister and I were at his bedside when he started having another coughing fit, and suddenly couldn't breathe at all. A thick mucus plug from his lungs had become lodged in his airway. We were rushed out of the room while the nurses rushed in and worked to revive him.

Dad was taken to ICU, and we all spent the weekend in the hospital, while we waited and prayed for him to wake up and the doctors tested for brain function. When Monday came, our family had to face the fact that he would not be coming back to us. After an excruciating family meeting, we told the doctors to disconnect him from the respirator. He wouldn't want to live that way. Eerily, he actually told Mitch that he was going to die on the day he had his accident that early August morning. We had to let him go. He was moved up to the oncology wing, and for the next four days we took turns sitting with him and nurturing each other. Finally, on the fourth day, Dad left us.

A few days later, I took Mom and Dad back to their home in southern Washington State. Mom sat in the seat beside me as I drove, while Dad (whose remains were by now inside the mahogany cremation urn) was strapped securely into the seatbelt in the back seat of their Buick. Mom and I agreed he would want to have his seatbelt on.

When Mom got up the next morning, she just sat in her chair at the kitchen table and wondered what she was going to do without Dad. After fifty-two years together, she was lost at the thought of living without him. Leaving her there in her grief to return home with my husband was a really hard thing to do. I didn't leave Mom there alone. My brother and his wife were then living on the property, in the apartment my dad built in the front of the barn for my maternal grandfather. Mitch and his wife did the best they could to accommodate her needs, and keep up with the maintenance on the family property, but after four years it was time to move on. They deserved more of their own life together, having only been married for a couple of years and being Mom's helpers and watchers for all of that time.

Understandably, Mom had a hard time letting go. She agreed it was time to move, as she knew the home, yard and pasture was too much for her and Mitch to keep up with. We sold the house, and then used the proceeds to buy her a home near mine. As the oldest daughter, it was only natural for me to take on this role in the family, just as my mother did for her parents.

The purpose of my story is not to freak you out or make you sad or worried about what might happen with your own elders. Life's a crapshoot. You take your chances every day. When that moment comes, you'll do what you have to do. As it relates to being involved in someone else's medical care, what Benjamin Disraeli said is good advice: "I am prepared for the worst, but hope for the best."

My goal with this book is to help you be prepared, as best you can, for what may be ahead of you as a caregiver for someone you care about. If you know what information you need to have, and a bit about what to expect when your loved one needs medical care, you can make the journey easier for all involved.

One generation to the next, our roles in life evolve from being cared for as children, to having our own children that we care for, to caring for our parents when they become more like children again. Back in the day, when Grandma and Grandpa needed care, they moved in with their kids and were cared for by family, an old country doctor, and homemade remedies until they died. Those were the norms at the time. In 1900, life expectancy in the United States was 46 years for men and 48 years for women. Today, life expectancy for both men and women is closer to 80. That leaves many more years for seniors to be cared for, and today's environment for that care is completely different than in your Grandma's time.

An article on the University of Missouri Extension website says that the average American woman will spend eighteen years providing some kind of care and assistance to an elderly family member. Family members provide approximately 80 percent of the necessary care for the elderly, and most often, the single primary caregiver is an adult daughter or spouse. Longer life spans means that caregivers often balance care of their own children with care of Mom and Dad, along with both spouses having careers, the infamous sandwich generation. Chances are, you will serve in a caregiving role at some point in your life. I didn't pick when I became a caregiver, it just happened. Life happens, things change, and one day out of the blue you may get "the call" and down the path you go.

THE CALL…

The call can come at any time, and for an unimaginable number of reasons. My experience is that it often comes in the middle of the night, but that's probably just my luck. Every situation is different, and the last one cannot predict the next one. If your family member requiring care is a senior, there will be a next time, until whichever one is the last time. I don't mean to sound unfeeling, just honest. The call can originate from any number of places, like when the assisted living facility you just moved Uncle Harry into calls to say they are sending him to the hospital with chest pains. The hospital may call and tell you that Grandma has taken a turn for the worse, and you should come. There's always a call in a crisis.

Unlike the call I received when my dad had his accident, not all calls end in disaster. A couple of years ago, on a 4th of July weekend, I got a call from my mother at about 10 P.M. When the phone rang, I was in my pajamas, comfortably sleeping in my recliner, next to my husband who was also dozing in front of the television. I had seen Mom earlier in the day, and knew she wasn't feeling well. She was in the middle of a course of antibiotics, prescribed for a urinary tract infection, and her body was rebelling with a horrible case of diarrhea. By the time she called me, she had fitfully slept most of the day in between trips to the bathroom and she was so miserable, she didn't know what to do for herself. She was scared and so she called me to come over and help her.

This is what happened in the next ninety minutes. I got out of my chair, changed clothes, got in the car, and headed to Mom's. About halfway there, I got into a fender bender when a sixteen year old kid, with a brand new license, didn't watch where he was going and drove into my left, rear quarter panel. I quickly exchanged insurance information with his father, who had been in the car ahead of him and saw what had happened. After explaining briefly why I was in such a hurry, I jumped back in my crunched car and continued on to Mom's house.

I arrived at Mom's to find her curled up in her bed, with the dog at her side, wishing it would all just go away. Her biggest problem was that she couldn't stop pooping. I asked her if she wanted to go to the hospital, and she refused. So I left her house, ran to Walgreen's, and bought some Immodium®. Upon my return, I gave her a dose of the anti-diarrheal medicine, had her drink a full glass of water while I watched, checked her blood sugar, tucked her into bed, kissed her on the head and said I'd be back in the morning. I also told her that if she wasn't markedly better, she was going to ER. I then got back into my car, and drove home. As I sat down to tell my husband what had happened, I looked at the clock and couldn't believe it had only been an hour and a half since my butt left my recliner when the phone rang. How did that happen? Every crisis and call has its own story.

So just what do you do when the phone rings in the middle of the night? I know you've heard it a million times, but the necessity of staying calm is at the top of the list in a crisis. That's because it is both true and important. The first thing you need to do is take a deep breath, and listen carefully to the caller, to make sure you understand what you are hearing. Especially if you are awakening from a deep sleep, you need to clear your head and repeat back the information you are hearing, to confirm you are clearly comprehending it all. Even if it's in the middle of the day, and you're just doing laundry when that phone rings, you're not expecting the conversation you are about to have. In a crisis, take that deep breath and ensure you are fully present so you can engage and act in turn. I know your immediate instinct might be to run out the door in your pajamas, leaving the front door wide open, as you head for the car. Resist the urge and try to be calm.

The next step is to start asking more questions. This is an opportunity to do your own phone based triage of sorts, to determine the urgency of the crisis, and establish what steps need to be taken first. Those questions will differ depending who made the call and what the emergency is, but here are some of the scenarios you might encounter.

THE CALL COMES FROM MOM AT HOME

Here are some questions you might ask when you get the call from the person actually having the crisis or someone who is physically with them as it is happening.

Is the person unconscious?
- Do they have chest pain?
- Are they having difficulty breathing?

- Is there severe abdominal pain?
- Is there bleeding?
- Are they in severe pain from a fall or other problem?
- Have they sustained a burn that is bigger than the size of a hand?
- Are they choking?
- Are they having convulsions?

If the answer to any of these questions is yes, call 911. If you're unsure, call anyway. The dispatcher will help you assess the situation, and tell you if EMS is needed or not.

Here's a list of the questions the dispatcher will need answered in order to get the right kind of help to you quickly. Make sure the person making the call can answer these questions. If the person who called you cannot quickly answer these questions and you can, even if you are not there you should make the call.

The location of the emergency, including street address and cross streets.

- The phone number you are calling from, and/or a phone number where the emergency is taking place, if you are not there yet.
- The nature of your emergency, which will include the answers to the questions above.
- The age of the person. If you're not sure, guess.
- Do they have any existing medical conditions?

Do your best to keep everyone as calm as you can. Every minute will seem like an eternity, but it feels that way because of the uncertainty and possibly pain. If you remain as calm as you can muster, the person experiencing the crisis will be more likely to remain calmer as well. You can always freak out later, if you need to!

You can avoid much of the delay and confusion of relaying important medical information through a third party like an EMS dispatcher or on site EMS personnel when they arrive by having a Vial of Life in your elder's home. This is a nationwide program; they provide you with a form, you then print and fill out, recording all the pertinent medical information about your senior. The form includes vital statistics like height, weight, birth date and such, and also has a place to note if Mom has specific problems like trouble with hearing or seeing. There is a place for recording medications, including allergies to medications taken in the past, and chronic conditions the patient suffers from such as diabetes, Alzheimer's, or congestive heart failure. Once the form is filled out, you put it in a plastic zip top bag, and stick it on the front or side of the refrigerator. This is free assistance. They also provide stickers for you to put on your entry doors so that EMS will know to look for the Vial of Life upon arrival. Here is the link for the website - http://www.vialoflife.com/.

WHEN THE CALL COMES FROM A CARE FACILITY

As the emergency contact for anyone receiving care in an assisted living community, or a skilled nursing facility, you will have occasion to deal with staff calling to tell you, "Uncle Dan is being transported to the hospital. You can meet them there."

By the time you get the call, the staff at the facility has already been dealing with the problem, and have determined that, based on Uncle Dan's medical condition and the regulations at their facility, he needs more care than they can provide. The person who makes that call to you may or may not know all that is happening medically, they could simply be the messenger. Get what information you can, and get more details when you get to the hospital.

When a resident is transported to the hospital from a nursing home or assisted living facility, the EMS responders should receive a packet of information containing a complete medication list, and other information that will assist medical staff in understanding the patient's history, including any pre-existing conditions they need to be aware of. You will want to ask about it when you arrive at the hospital. Be prepared with a current medication list, if you have it, just in case.

WHEN THE CALL COMES FROM THE HOSPITAL

When my mother-in-law was in the final years of her life, she suffered from congestive heart failure, among other maladies at over 90 years of age, and was in and out of the hospital several times as her disease progressed and her heart grew weaker. The calls we would get were often informing us she had taken a turn for the worse, and if we wanted to see her again, we should come now. This is never the call you want to receive. We received this type of call many times before she passed at ninety-four, and she recovered from all but one of these episodes.

As the saying goes, it's not over until it's over. My husband and I sat many hours on what we thought might be a "death watch," and turned out not so. My point is, getting a call like this one does not always mean your worst fears are coming true. Modern medicine can do wondrous things. In the end, only God knows when the last time will come.

When the worst call comes, again, do your best to remain calm and do what you need to do. When you arrive at the bedside of your loved one, be aware that your calm and positive attitude will be the comfort they need and it will help you be more present, as well. I know it's hard when you are afraid they're going to die any minute but even if that's true, you don't want to bring unpleasant energy into that room with you. Take time for a couple of good, deep breaths before you walk into the room. If you start to lose it, excuse yourself for a few minutes. Even if they're unconscious or sleeping, the energy you bring to the room is your responsibility, so make it as positive and loving as you can.

Dr. Jill Bolte Taylor, a Harvard-trained and published brain scientist, who studied the nervous system, had a severe hemorrhage in the left hemisphere of her own brain in 1996. She was not yet fifty. On the afternoon of this stroke, she could not walk, talk, read, write, or recall any of her life up to that point. During her recovery, although she had lost the ability to speak, she could keenly feel the energy that each of the nurses, doctors, friends and family brought to her room as she fought to recover. As Dr. Jill says, "Take responsibility for the energy you bring," and it certainly applies when entering the room of anyone who is sick especially if they are near death. It took eight years for her to completely recover all of her physical function and thinking ability, and she is now author of the New York Times bestselling memoir, *My Stroke of Insight: A Brain Scientist's Personal Journey* (2008, Viking Penguin). She has also given a couple of TED talks. Here is the link to one of those talks - http://www.ted.com/speakers/jill_bolte_taylor.

NOT EVERY CALL IS A HOSPITAL EMERGENCY

Wherever the call originates, it means, as a caregiver or concerned family member, there is a next step. Your triage questions should help you decide if the call requires a visit to the hospital then and there. Maybe you can simply go check on Mom, like I did right after colliding with a rookie driver, and wait until morning to either see her regular doctor or make a trip to the urgent care clinic. Dealing with a non-emergent health problem can be readily addressed by many urgent care clinics, and will cost less money and time than a visit to the hospital emergency room.

Below is a list of medical issues that can easily be handled by an urgent care clinic, if you have one available:

Minor accidents and falls

- Sprains and strains
- Moderate back problems
- Breathing difficulties (i.e. mild to moderate asthma)
- Bleeding/cuts not bleeding profusely, but requiring stitches
- Diagnostic services, including X-rays and laboratory tests
- Eye irritation and redness
- Fever or flu
- Vomiting, diarrhea or dehydration
- Severe sore throat or cough
- Minor broken bones and fractures (i.e. fingers, toes)
- Skin rashes and infections
- Urinary tract infections

On the other hand, if you called 911 or are transporting your Dad directly to the hospital for a more emergent situation, you will be at the beginning of a journey through the health care machine through the emergency room. The first time is especially stressful at best, and can be overwhelming at times. The following chapters will help you step through the process, and give you an idea of what to expect with an elderly or sick person. The more you know, the less you have to worry about what you don't know. Less worry is good.

CHAPTER TWO:
AN EMERGENCY ROOM VISIT

*We could never learn to be brave and patient,
if there were only joy in the world.*
~ Helen Keller

The call has come, and whatever crisis is in process has developed into a walk into the mouth of the machine the hospital emergency room. If your crisis required a call to 911, and Mom has been transported by ambulance, you will need to go to the reception desk, identify yourself, and let them know Mom is or will be arriving by ambulance. Depending on your situation and distance from the hospital, you may arrive before the EMS unit does. Be patient, they will be there shortly even if it seems crazy that you have arrived before the ambulance. They are supposed to get to the hospital fast, but fast is relative, just like a lot of other things. They are also responsible for stabilizing the patient at the beginning of the journey, and during transport. If Mom isn't there yet, you'll still need to complete a check-in process, and wait until she is assigned a treatment room, before you can go back to see her.

If you're transporting Mom or Dad to the ER, the first challenge will be getting them into the building. Many seniors have a difficult enough time getting around when they're well, and being sick puts them at an even greater risk for falling, becoming disoriented, or panicking. Minimize the amount of walking they have to do. Most hospitals are set up so that you can pull up close to the emergency door, acquire a wheelchair if necessary, and escort your patient inside. Get Mom inside first, and if possible, let the receptionist know she is there and that you'll be back after parking the car. Some hospitals offer valet service; take advantage of it if that is available. After reading this paragraph, you may see the up side to calling an ambulance in a crisis situation if Mom or Dad's mobility is an issue. If in doubt, make the call and have EMS provide transport. The other upside to the ambulance is that EMS will begin providing care and close, continuous monitoring immediately.

WHAT TO HAVE WHEN YOU GET THERE

When you check in, you'll need to provide basic information about why you are there, who is being treated, their primary care physician's name, and what kind of insurance, if any, will be paying the bill. If you don't have this information, it doesn't mean you won't be seen. They may want to take copies of insurance cards if you have them available. It's a good idea to take the time to have copies of these documents and identification cards in your possession.

Before my mother moved to assisted living at age 83, she took more than one ambulance ride directly from her house to the hospital. I met her over there. I keep my insurance cards in my purse, and so does she. It isn't surprising that she doesn't have her purse with her when she arrives by ambulance, because it was left behind in dealing with the emergency. I keep my own copy of her information, so I don't have to worry about this situation anymore. Do yourself a favor, and plan ahead for these basic things. At a minimum, you will want to be able to provide the name of the company, policy and member/group numbers to the receptionist when you arrive in the emergency room. If your loved one has Medicare or Medicaid, that will most likely be their primary insurance. They may also have a supplement or secondary insurance in addition. You'll want to ask Mom about that too when you're putting together your Vial of Life packet or whatever organizational tool you are using to capture this information.

If you've been at the same hospital before, they may have patient information on file, and simply ask you if it is still current. If you have a Vial of Life packet, bring or keep a copy of it with you. Most of the information you will need to check in completely is recorded on it. Before I knew about Vial of Life, I made up my own list. Here is a link to my website where you can print it out and fill in the blanks - jackiemcdaniels.com.

Now that you're at the hospital, where Mom can get the medical attention she needs, your next step is to wait. Yep, you just drove across town like a crazy person, trying to arrive in the shortest possible time. Once you arrive, you're asked to wait. Get used to it, you could be there awhile, waiting at different stages of the visit. According to ProPublica, an independent, non-profit organization that produces investigative journalism in the public interest, as of December of 2013, the national average wait time to see a doctor in the emergency room is twenty-eight minutes. If you're treated and discharged, the average wait time is one hundred and thirty-eight minutes. If you are admitted, add an additional ninety-seven minutes to be taken to a room.

NAVIGATING TRIAGE – THE ASSESSMENT PROCESS

What are you waiting for first? You're waiting for Mom to go through triage, to have a nurse determine the seriousness of her problem. The emergency room staff has three goals: to assess, diagnose and treat the current medical complaint. Triage is the assessment part of the triangle. Usually, a registered emergency room nurse will have the duty of evaluating incoming patients to determine who needs to be seen in which order. There may also be a CNA (Certified Nurse Assistant) who will take readings of Mom's body temperature, pulse rate (or heart rate), blood pressure, respiratory rate and oxygen saturation, collectively referred to as vitals. These readings give the nurses and doctors some immediate clues to the patient's general condition. These will become a part of the medical records, or chart, for this emergency visit. Once the treatment begins, these vitals will be taken, ideally, about every hour. In the meantime, you'll continue to wait until you can be assigned a treatment room.

How long you will wait depends on the severity of Mom's medical issue, and how many other patients are ahead of you in triage. It also may vary depending on the day of the week, the size of the hospital, the availability of other hospitals in the area, which means lots of things you have no control over. For peace of mind, your best bet is to get over that loss of control right away.

Patients suffering from shortness of breath and chest pain will be seen first. Be aware, unlike being on hold with the customer service department of your cell phone carrier, you will not necessarily be served in the order you arrived. In addition to patients waiting in the emergency area with you, there may be patients arriving in ambulances. If you and your senior were able to walk into the hospital, you likely have a less serious problem than if you arrived by ambulance. Keep that in mind as you wait.

I often have to remind Mom that there may be people sicker than she is ahead of her. Patience is not her strong suit, and when any of us are feeling sick, everything takes too long. My reminder about other people in greater need usually kicks her kind heart into gear, and she forgets about how long we've been waiting, for a while anyway. Having a few items with you, like small bottles of water, a book or kindle, and maybe a pillow can make the time you and Mom wait a bit more bearable.

If Mom is not having a heart attack or bleeding profusely, and there are a number of other people waiting, you may have the opportunity to use the bathroom at this stage. My advice is that you do. Why? Because once you begin treatment, you will be inside the machine and in there, it feels as if the space time continuum changes. You can almost guarantee that if you wait until later, it will be the minute you leave that the doctor will come in with his findings. If you miss him, he may not be seen again for some time. Just take my word for it, and take the time to use the bathroom early in your visit.

IN THE TREATMENT ROOM

If Mom came in by ambulance, she'll go right to a treatment room, if one is available. Triage is considered handled by the EMS people, and they may have initiated some treatment, such as starting oxygen augmentation or IV fluids. If not, when your turn comes and treatment starts, there will be more medical intake process to complete. The information you provide at this step is crucial. There will be a Registered Nurse assigned as Mom's primary nurse. Make sure to get his or her name, remember the face and keep it in mind this is your best friend in this scary place. Although he or she is probably responsible for several rooms and patients, the nurse is generally your most accessible staff member in the emergency department. It takes a special person to be an emergency nurse. They see people at their worst, most times, and endure far more than simple rudeness while doing a very tough job.

The nurse will ask a million questions about Mom's medical history. In the meantime, a nurse's assistant, CNA, or other qualified staff member will begin taking Mom's vitals, again. The more accurate the answers to the nurse's questions, the sooner the medical team can provide the appropriate treatment. The questions will likely start with basic information about Mom's symptoms. The nurse will direct her questions to Mom, as is appropriate. Always let Mom take a shot at answering the questions first. It's important for her state of mind to be evaluated as well as her other symptoms. If Mom is not giving the right answers to the questions, you need to speak up. Also, this process will go much faster if you keep Mom on track with talking about her current problem, and the most relevant background, not the arthritic knee she predicts the weather with or other historical anecdotes.

The nurse will also evaluate Mom's level of pain. The standard question is, "On a scale of one to ten, with ten being the worst pain you have ever felt and one being mild discomfort, what is your pain level right now?" It seems like a simple enough question when the nurse rattles it off, as she has probably already done many times that shift. If you've been in an emergency room, you may remember the poster in the treatment rooms that show ten faces ranging from smiles to tears. Patients under severe stress from pain or illness, particularly if they are a senior, can have difficulty answering this question, because it is abstract. It's not that they don't know if they're in pain but they may have a hard time processing the question. Think about it, there are four different concepts to consider in the question:

1. Scale of one to ten - Mom thinks, "Okay, between one and ten. Got that".

2. Ten being the most pain you have ever felt - "What is the most pain I have ever felt? Was it when broke my wrist, or when I fell off the ladder and skinned my leg bad that time? Hmm, I think it was the ladder. Okay. I don't feel that bad."

3. One being mild discomfort - "Is that like a headache."

4. What is your level of pain now? – By this time, they may be confused and in pain as well. "What was the question?"

You get the picture. I often have to repeat an edited version of the question to Mom, speaking more slowly and often a bit louder to get a meaningful response. If a patient isn't responding appropriately a nurse may ask questions like, "Do you know where you are? What is the date today? Who is the president?" Responses to these questions reveal a lot to practitioners about what a patient's mental abilities might be. Please let them answer these questions without help. Seniors in this strained state of mind can easily find their memory and communication skills are more compromised than usual. Listen carefully to what they say, and try not to coach them into correct answers. Clarify answers that are vague or incomplete. Do speak up if you see a marked difference in their abilities from what is normal for them that may suggest an additional emergent symptom of the current crisis. The more information the doctors and nurses get up front, the better job they can do to diagnose and treat whatever is going on.

MEDICATION COMMUNICATION

After a general assessment, the nurse will want to know about medications. You can go several ways with this. If you can easily collect the medicines Mom takes on a regular basis, and take them with you, that works well. Make sure you bring only the medication she is currently taking. If you bring a bunch of old prescription bottles with drugs that she isn't taking any more, it can really confuse the situation. Nurses and doctors know what the drugs are used for, and may therefore assume the patient has and is being treated for whatever that drug treats. For example, say Mom used to take Lipitor for high cholesterol but she lost some weight and cleaned up her diet a bit, and now she doesn't take it anymore. If you bring in a bottle of Lipitor, doctors could assume she has heart disease from high cholesterol and focus on that when her real issue is actually something else. The other way to go is to keep a list like the Vial of Life form or whatever you have chosen to use. You can see why it is also important you keep this list up to date.

There's even an app for that. Of course, there is. There are smartphone apps with features that allow you to record information, and then give you access to medical records and medication information that are securely stored in the cloud, or you can store on your own. These apps are available for both iPhone and Android devices. You can also use your phone to store a text file of medications in a note format or similar using word processing software or applications. Taking a photo of the list you made up for Mom or the Vial of Life packet and storing it on your phone works, or take a photo of each of the current medication bottles, just be sure to keep this mobile repository up to date as well.

Once the intake process is complete, it's time to don the hospital gown. The actual diagnosis part of this journey doesn't begin until the patient is wearing the fancy, cotton gown with the ties in the back and snaps on the shoulders. If you're the caregiver or advocate for your dad, Uncle Dan or your next-door neighbor Pete, don't hesitate to ask the nurse or assistant to help him while you step outside. That way you protect your dignity and his. I think men have an especially hard time being in the emergency room or the hospital because being sick makes them feel weak, physically and mentally. Although none of us like to feel weak, for most men this is really uncomfortable. (Not to leave out you loving and dedicated male caregivers, if you're with mom, or Aunt Susie, being aware of her modesty about her body will be much appreciated.) Once the gown is on, you'll be in wait mode again. This time you are waiting for a doctor.

The emergency room can feel cold in varied ways, from the room temperature itself to the rather direct way personal questions are asked like, "When was the last time you had a bowel movement?" One of the few comforting things for Mom when she is in the emergency room is a warm blanket. I always ask for one once she is in her gown, and most of the time nurses are happy to provide this small comfort. However, if Mom is running a fever, only light blankets are allowed. Likewise, if Mom wants water, ask for this first.

Soon, there will be a parade of different providers and technicians that begin to arrive. Remembering your nurse's name and face is advisable because he or she is your communication connection to the actual emergency room physician that will be treating your loved one. If you have a question or concern, and don't know who to ask for or what she looks like walking down the corridor, you may spend much more time waiting and becoming frustrated.

The nurse will likely begin connecting Mom to the patient monitor, which tracks most of the vital signs I talked about earlier. She will often leave the blood pressure cuff on, and the monitor will activate the cuff periodically. The nurse will also put a pulse oximeter on Mom's finger to monitor her oxygen saturation. If Mom is having trouble breathing, or if the oxygen saturation reading taken during triage is below normal levels of 95 – 100, the nurse may start giving her oxygen by placing a nasal cannula on her face, under her nose. The elderly are chronic shallow breathers, especially when they aren't feeling good, so don't be alarmed by this. My mother, like most patients, dislikes having the oxygen on because it really dries her nasal passages and sinuses. I know from experience that she is a shallow breather, so if the oximeter reading is a bit low, I ask Mom to take a couple of good deep breaths and her numbers will come back up. It's also very common for them to run an electrocardiogram to check heart function if they have any concerns about heart malfunctions.

There will most likely be a phlebotomist from the lab who will take blood samples. They always want blood to analyze. A very common problem for seniors is a urinary tract infection. A blood test will show too many white blood cells if an infection is present. Certain types of proteins are released into the blood during a heart attack. A blood test can measure these proteins. Blood tells many tales. If you, as a caregiver have a problem seeing needles and blood, it would be best if you either look away, or step out of the room entirely for a moment. No one needs to be picking you up off the floor if you pass out, and you aren't going to be doing your senior much good that way either.

There may be someone from the intake desk who comes to the room to have you verify your insurance information, and to give you a copy of your Medicare Rights and a paper to sign that verifies they gave it to you. You can also ask them about a HIPAA release form. HIPAA stands for the **Health Insurance Portability & Accountability Act** of 1996, a federal law that protects personal medical information, and recognizes the rights to relevant medical information of family caregivers and others directly involved in providing or paying for care.

You should have one of these HIPAA release forms, signed by the person you are caring for, on file with every practitioner you visit. You can list yourself and multiple family members or close friends on the form so if your sister calls from out of town, they will be able to share pertinent medical info. Without it, doctors and nurses are required by law not to discuss medical information without the patient's consent. This point is covered if you are standing in the room with your family member when the doctor discusses what he thinks is going on, while the patient is present and not objecting to the information being shared.

MEETING THE EMERGENCY DOCTOR – OBTAINING A DIAGNOSIS

At some point in time, someone will pass through the door and introduce themselves as your doctor or attending physician. He or she will probably begin asking a lot of the same questions you have already answered. Whatever you told the nurse during triage may or may not have been put in front of the doctor before they walk into the treatment room. Be patient, just like most of the other people you have encountered since you entered the building, the doctor is seeing to multiple patients at a time. Cut him or her some slack, and don't mention how long you have been waiting.

It's best to be direct and brief while describing whatever symptoms brought you and Mom to the hospital this time. Although the doctor may need to be aware of the laundry list of maladies Mom is being treated for at 85, he or she only needs details about why Mom is here for this visit. Sometimes, seniors have a tendency to talk a lot, especially if they live alone and don't get many chances to tell someone about all their aches and pains. You may have to rein her in and prompt her back to the topic at hand.

TREATMENT PLANS: TO ADMIT OR NOT TO ADMIT THAT IS THE QUESTION

The emergency doctor will diagnose whatever problem Mom came in with, and determine if she needs further tests, what treatment is necessary, and if she needs to be admitted to the hospital for her care. In many cases the emergency doctor will contact the primary care doctor for his or her opinion. When they decide what to do, orders will be written by one of them that dictates how things will proceed. You must have doctors' orders to move on to the next step, which is treatment, and this means either out the door to be discharged, or upstairs to a room to be admitted. It doesn't matter which other providers you speak to, it's the doctors' "orders" that will move you along in the process.

If whatever illness or accident brought you into the ER can be bandaged up, stitched up, relieved by IV fluids or a prescription, you get your walking papers and are sent out the door with follow-up instructions. Patients are expected to follow up with their regular doctor, specialist or pharmacy as indicated on your discharge papers. If things are more serious than that, it's on to admission you go and into inner workings of the machine.

Most times when Mom has required a trip to the emergency room, she has been admitted. In her case, she is prone to urinary tract infections. (This is very common for seniors.) She is also an insulin-dependent diabetic and thin as a rail in her 5'3" frame. She would weigh in at one hundred pounds clothed and soaking wet. When she gets one of these infections, her blood sugars get so high that her glucose meter only registers "Hi," which means it's over 500. Normal fasting blood sugars should be between 70 -99. High blood sugars, as well as infections, cause the body to release lots of urine to try to expel excess glucose and infection out of the system. This often results in dehydration, with symptoms of weakness, dizziness and confusion. When Mom is in this condition, there is no question she needs to be admitted. She can barely sit up. But I have had to wait with her for several hours, so that the doctor can observe how she is responding to treatment, before he or she will decide to admit her or not.

Sometimes patients may in fact be stable enough to be discharged but because they live alone, and don't have someone to look after them, they are admitted. This is a good thing in many ways, and emergency personnel will usually inquire about a senior's living arrangement before they make a decision to admit or discharge them. In some cases, they may be kept at the hospital for a short time for observation only. Some hospitals have specific units for this purpose. These units can be a stop-gap for those that need it, but be aware, if the doctor thinks they may need to be observed for say twenty-four hours, charges billed to Medicare will be as an outpatient instead of inpatient, and coverage is very different and charges will be more expensive. If your senior's emergency doctor decides to admit them, ask if he is expecting them to be in the hospital for at least two days. If the answer is yes, Medicare Part A will cover their percentage of hospital expenses, and if they require skilled nursing care after a hospital stay for either rehab to get them back on their feet and independent again, or for further, less critical, treatment to heal from a traumatic health event Medicare will cover time in a skilled facility up to their maximum of one hundred days for each benefit period. Generous, aren't they? Here are the specific coverage requirements from the NOLO Law for All website:

"Despite the common misconception that nursing homes are covered by Medicare, the truth is that it covers only a limited amount of inpatient skilled nursing care. For each spell of illness, Medicare will cover only a total of 100 days of inpatient care in a skilled nursing facility, and then only if your doctor continues to prescribe skilled nursing care or therapy."

For the first 20 of 100 days, Medicare will pay for all covered costs, which include all basic services but not television, telephone, or private room charges. For the next 80 days, the patient is personally responsible for a daily copayment, and Medicare pays the rest of covered costs. In 2013, the copayment amount is $148; the amount goes up each year.

After 100 days in any benefit period, you are on your own as far as Medicare Part A hospital insurance is concerned. (Lifetime reserve days, available for hospital coverage, do not apply to a stay in a nursing facility.) However, if you later begin a new spell of illness (called a benefit period), your first 100 days in a skilled nursing facility will again be covered.

All of this is quite convoluted and hard to track when someone is ill, but being aware of these guidelines may help you, as a caregiver, to help your senior avoid unnecessary charges that most of those on fixed incomes can't afford.

DOCUMENTS YOU SHOULD HAVE ON FILE

I left this part until the end for a reason. No one wants to talk about what happens if Mom stops breathing, her heart stops beating, or she loses brain function. End of life planning is a tough subject for everyone. There are three very important documents you should have copies of, if you are acting as the primary caregiver for a loved one. These are Advanced Directives or Living Will, a Medical Durable Power of Attorney, and a POLST form if appropriate. I think most people ignore the importance of these documents, because they require us to entertain the possibility that one of your visits to the hospital with your loved one will be the last one. Looking at our mortality is always difficult, but one of those hard facts in life.

Living wills and advance directives describe a person's preferences for end-of-life care. These documents speak for them when they're not able to speak for themselves. As family caregivers, we need to be aware of what our loved one's wishes are. Although it's not an easy conversation to have, you must have it. Put yourself in their place, and think about what you would want if something unexpected and incapacitating happened to you, like becoming trapped under a riding lawn mower.

My first real experience in dealing with these questions was when my dad had his accident and was in the hospital in Spokane. The day after the transfer from the Tri-Cities, where his accident happened, my sister Lori was sitting with him when the chaplain came in to see him and check in with his family. The chaplains are a good resource in the hospital, and can be a true blessing if you and your family find yourselves there with a critically ill loved one. The chaplain asked Lori if Dad had a living will, and she didn't know. She told him he would have to talk to me, or my mother. Unfortunately, it wasn't something we had discussed before the accident happened, and none of us were ready for it. The chaplain spoke to my sister for a few minutes, and left the forms for advanced directives in the room, so that we could look them over and fill them out later.

You can imagine how difficult it was to broach this topic with my mother, as her husband of fifty-two years lay in a hospital bed with more tubes in him than you can count, being pumped full of morphine around the clock to ease the pain of 2nd and 3rd degree burns, and this makes him so foggy that he doesn't always know where is. When determining survival odds for burn victims, they calculate the TBSA (total body surface area) percentage (Dad's was about eight percent), add that to the patient's age, seventy-two, then add in a few points for complications of pre-existing health problems, like Parkinson's disease. Let's just say his chances of survival were not very good coming in the door. How do you ask your Mom if Dad told her his wishes for when he dies? I have no memory of what I actually said to her. She may have tried to talk to Dad about it, but he was only lucid in short spurts. At the time, we still had hope that he would recover from his injuries.

When it was all said and done, God made most of the decision for us, and family discussion decided the rest. I'm blessed to have a family that can have this kind of discussion without added drama. That's not the case for every family, which is why it's such a good idea to take care of this long before you need it.

Since then, I have made sure I have an advanced directive for my mother, so I don't have to wonder what the answer to the chaplain's question will be when her time comes. Advanced directives forms can differ from state to state. Check out this link to the American Bar Association for more discussion of these forms, and how you can get one for your state. Their Commission on Law and Aging section has very good information and resources to help you with the legal documents you need to prepare.

The other legal document your loved one should have is a Durable Medical Power of Attorney for Health Care. It goes by different names in different states, but serves the same purpose. The document designates a specific person or alternate to make medical decisions for a patient if they are unable to make them on their own. Choose this person carefully, based on the belief that they will carry out your wishes. I am the designated "Agent" for my Mom because I am here and available, but my sister is the alternate in case I cannot be reached in an emergent situation.

Two more advanced directives that you may have heard about are a Do Not Resuscitate (DNR) and a Physician's Order for Life Sustaining Treatment (POLST). These are similar documents with a few subtle differences. A DNR can be a part of someone's advanced directives. Advanced directives tell others what you want and don't want for end-of-life treatment, "should you at some time in the future become incapacitated." These are prepared by the patient with cooperation of his or her family. A POLST form is completed by your physician based on your "current physical condition." Remember how important physician orders can be? POLST forms can and should be updated if your current physical status changes.

If Mom is still at home alone and has a POLST in place, it should be indicated on her Vial of Life form or a sign near her bed, in case she has to call 911. In the hospital, a POLST notice may be placed above the patient's bed. Different states have different ways of handling these types of forms. To find out more about POLST in your state go to www.polst.org/. If hospital or EMS personnel don't know about a POLST or DNR order they are obligated to attempt resuscitation of a patient they are called to help. They are trained to save people's lives, not let them die. Make sure they know your loved one's wishes. For example, my Mom has a DNR section in her Advanced Directives and a POLST on file with her doctor, the assisted living facility where she lives, and on file with the hospital. As a widow for fourteen years and nearly 85 years of age, Mom is ready to let go of this life whenever God decides it's her time. She's good with that, and has let us know what she wants and doesn't want when the time comes.

As a caregiver, having these decisions made ahead of time takes away the uncertainty that comes with questions that begin with, "What if ____." Even if the conversation is hard to initiate, there is no question it's a conversation worth having in the beginning of a relationship between a caregiver and her charge, whether they are a relative or not. If your charge is not a relative, encourage them to have the discussion with their family if that is more appropriate. Every caregiving situation is different.

WHEN MOM IS BEING ADMITTED

Now that you know Mom is going to be staying in the hospital for at least two midnights, you can feel a bit of relief that there will be someone there constantly to watch over her. This is a good thing, and always a relief for me to know I can go home and take care of my own life and family without the constant worry of what is going on with Mom. That said, even though she's been admitted, there are still many things you can do that will help her get the best care while she is there. No one should be in the hospital completely alone. Everyone needs an advocate while being in the bowels of the medical machine. The next chapter will help you make the best of a hospital visit for your senior, and get them back to wellness.

CHAPTER THREE:
ADMISSION-WHAT HAPPENS NOW?

Bound by paperwork, short on hands, sleep, and energy...
nurses are rarely short on caring.
~ Sharon Hudacek, A Daybook for Nurses

DECIDING TO MAKE A BREAK FOR IT

As a caregiver, you can't be there around the clock, even if you think you should be or want to be. I can't tell you how many hours I have spent waiting for a room once the doctors have decided to keep one of my loved ones in the hospital. Our local hospital has just over two hundred fifty beds, and is the largest medical campus in north Idaho and western Montana. Very often, the hospital census (the current count of admitted patients) is high. Even after the admitting decision, we have to wait for someone else to get their discharge order, actually leave the room, and then the room must be cleaned and prepared for a new patient. Just because the doctors have decided to admit a patient, doesn't mean they actually have a bed to put them in just yet. Be sure to ask how long the wait is expected to be. Expect it to be longer than you are told, because it will feel that way anyway, and you have already been waiting for hours by this point.

In a perfect world, I could step away during this time, and there would be someone else who could sit with Mom while she waits to be moved, just so she wouldn't have to be alone. My siblings live out of town, and I am currently the only one with the job description of caregiver in our family, so there is seldom a backup available. I know that I need to deal with the imperfect scenario more often than not, so I usually take this portion of the waiting time as an opportunity to take a break, breathe some fresh air, make a few phone calls with the "Mom Report," and even get myself something to eat. By this point in the journey, the emergency staff will have stabilized Mom's condition and continue to monitor her. A CNA will be in once an hour to check vitals, and Mom will be given the control to press for the nurse if she needs one.

In addition to taking care of someone, a caregiver's job also includes taking care of yourself. If someone you love is in the hospital, and you are acting as their advocate, you need to take whatever down time is available for self care. This is to preserve your emotional balance and your stamina, as these trips are taxing. For me, a trip to Starbucks is a must and thankfully it's just a couple of blocks from the hospital. I'm a coffee gal, and hospital coffee usually sucks. Whatever small pleasures will give you a few minutes of peace, and an opportunity to release the scary thoughts you've been entertaining for the past several hours, is good for you. Maybe your break includes calling your husband or partner for moral support, or a girlfriend, or checking in on your own son or daughter. However feels best for you, find a way to let go of some your stress. You have at least another round ahead of you, and even a prize fighter takes a break between rounds.

WHAT'S IN THE BAG - PACKING FOR COMFORT AND PRACTICALITY

Once Mom is moved to her room, there is usually an opportunity on that first day to run back to Mom's house to pack a bag. It's a really great idea to have a pre-packed hospital bag stashed away in the closet. This can be handy to give to the EMS staff to take with Mom if she needs to ride in an ambulance, and could include a copy of her Vial of Life forms with all her medical information. I was never that organized, but below is a list of things that are especially useful to have in this bag, pre-packed or not. Some of the items in the bag are for you, to refresh or pass time while tending to Mom's bedside:

- Toothbrushes / paste / denture case / cleaner
- Hairbrush/comb
- Light robe
- Slippers/non-skid socks
- Disposable briefs

- Glasses
- Hearing Aids / Extra Batteries
- Books / Puzzles / Music
- Bottled Water
- Crackers
- Hand Sanitizer
- Tissues
- List of phone contacts

THINGS TO LEAVE HOME

Leave all valuables at home, yours and Mom's. I don't leave Mom's purse or jewelry with her when she is admitted. There are many people in and out of a patient's room when they are in the hospital, most of whom are wonderful, honest people. Sometimes patients are moved from one room to another, and things get misplaced or left behind. It is not necessary for Mom to have most of these things during her stay, and it isn't worth the hassle and hard feelings if something bad happens, or items are damaged, misplaced or stolen. Just leave these things at home for everyone's peace of mind.

You may have noticed I did not include a night gown or pajamas. My experience is that being in the hospital is a messy experience, especially with elders. Hospital gowns end up with everything from remnants of food going in to food coming out. You bring it, you wash it, you carry it. Let the hospital take care of the gowns. I include the disposable briefs in Mom's hospital bag because the ones the hospital provides are not the most comfortable, and they are always huge. If your Mom, like mine, is a skinny little thing, having underwear that fits, disposable or not, is a simple comfort. Being in the hospital is anything but comfortable, so any little thing is appreciated.

INTEL AND INSIGHT – SHARING WHAT YOU KNOW WITH THE TREATMENT TEAM

When Mom's room is ready, a transport person will come to move her to her assigned location. I follow them, as we ride the "staff only" elevator and then wheel onto the floor and into a room, to be greeted by a nurse or CNA who is expecting our arrival. The next step is to get Mom checked in at her new location in the hospital. Her primary nurse, for this shift, will come in to ask a million questions, including some of the same questions asked and answered when we entered through emergency. I always stay with Mom until this intake process is complete. As a caregiver, you should be present for this, especially if your elder is at all compromised in their memory or communication skills, as my mother is now.

This is a great time to start building your relationship with the nurses and other workers on the floor. Be as honest and straightforward as possible in answering the intake questions. This is the time to let her know if Mom is hard of hearing or has vision problems, or any other issue that will affect their interaction and the nurse's expectations and instructions. Make her your friend and ally, and show your appreciation for the job she does. There will be nurses you just don't click with, and some you decide you don't even like be nice to them anyway. They are only there one shift at a time, and have many other patients to care for. They become your main contact point for any information about your loved one. When I call to check on Mom, I want them to have a pleasant memory of me. It will make them more likely to return my calls promptly, and provide me with the update I want on Mom's treatment progress and doctors' orders for further treatment or discharge.

MEDICATION MAMBO - THE DANCE OF CONSISTENCY BETWEEN DEPARTMENTS

At intake, the nurse will also go over the medication list with you again. If you have it in your handy hospital go-bag, it's easy to get to and verify that what she has is the same list and you should ask questions of each other if it is not. Many medication mistakes happen when the list that comes up from emergency is incomplete or lost. Hospital computer systems usually keep track of these things, but always be sure to double check. Sometimes, doctors discontinue medications on admission, to rule out symptoms and side effects. Make sure that if this happens, it is an intentional change and not inadvertent, as new issues could obviously arise from these changes. You'll want to closely review the medication list when you discharge as well, to make sure there isn't a similar misunderstanding. Your pharmacist is a fantastic resource to help you go over a medication list after leaving the hospital. I'll share more about this in the discharge section.

During one of my father-in-law's hospital stays, my husband and I noticed that he was acting strangely. He was more confused than he had been the day before. The nurses said his vitals were good, and he seemed stronger. They thought he was improving. Because they didn't really know Dad like we did, they just thought he was a sweet, but confused old man. What we knew, that the nurses didn't, was that previously when his body was fighting a urinary tract infection he became confused and acted strangely. Being familiar with Dad's medications, I asked if he was being given the prophylactic dose of Ciprofloxacin he had been taking to prevent his recurrent UTI's. It turned out that he wasn't, and sure enough, had developed an infection while an inpatient. The doctor then reinstated the medication to his inpatient regimen. This is an example of the need to continue to monitor medications on a regular basis, even during the time someone you love is in the hospital.

Intake also includes inventorying personal belongings, so be sure and list all the stuff you brought in the go-bag including glasses, hearing aids, and dentures. I also provide my contact information, so the staff can contact me with any changes in Mom's condition or questions. There is usually a white board that has the nurses' names, CNA's name, and doctors' names in the room. I can't say it's always kept up to date with the nurse and doctor contacts, but I also use it to write my own name and phone number, so it's equally handy for everyone.

Before you leave, find out when shift changes occur, so you know when the best time is for you to check up on your loved one. Nurses have a meeting between shifts to exchange information about patient status. They will not be available to take your call during this time so plan accordingly. If you expect to have family calling in to the hospital for updates, you will need to make sure the HIPAA form is complete with the names of all those you want the nurse to disclose information to, should they call or visit. If you can manage it, try to keep that list very short, and use a phone tree, text, email or social media channels to give updates to Mom's friends and family. Most of the time, they don't need the details, they just want to know how the patient is progressing. The fewer telephone calls nurses have to answer, the more time they have to spend with their patients.

HOSPITAL DIET, CHOICES, CHALLENGES AND CHEATING?

A key part of the intake process is making arrangements for meals. Depending on what condition your loved one is being treated for, some foods may be restricted. My Mom has once been so sick and weak with a urinary tract infection, and with out of control blood sugars, that she had to be on thickened liquids, even coffee, until she could be evaluated by speech therapy to determine if she could swallow without risk of choking. Some seniors need their foods ground up because they can't chew very well. Foods can be pureed, ground or chopped (referred to in hospital as "mechanical soft") to suit the patient's needs.

Everyone knows hospital food is not gourmet cuisine, but people must eat. A few years ago, our hospital instituted what they call "room service." This allows me to order for Mom off of a menu, just like you would from a hotel. The menu is limited, but she can choose what she likes at most any time during the day. Being sick, having a good appetite is certainly not guaranteed. Having more choice in what you are served can improve the desire to eat. Even if you don't order your loved one's meals, and they eat the standard fare, ask about having textures altered, if it will make it easier for them to eat enough. It is important to get fuel in them so their body can have energy to heal.

Ask the nurse about bringing in food from outside of the hospital. In most cases, it's all right, but if certain foods are being restricted, stick with what the hospital staff is telling you. Mom's special treat is a tall black Starbucks Americano and a warm chocolate cookie. I bring it around meal time, so I know she has insulin on board to cover it. I love seeing the smile on her face become surrounded by gooey, melted chocolate that I have to wipe from her chin. Sometimes I have to wait several days for her to be well enough to enjoy them, but the wait is worth it.

HOSPITAL WHO'S WHO - NURSES ROCK!

There are a lot of people scurrying around in a hospital ward. It makes you wonder what the heck are all these people doing, and which one of them do you talk to if you have a question or a request? There have been many times, while in this environment, that I have felt invisible as staff members walk by on their way to somewhere else. Knowing who is who, and which staff members are your best resources, will make your time there less stressful and your presence more helpful to your loved one.

For each shift, there will be a Charge Nurse who is responsible for managing, supervising and assisting the nursing staff, as well as providing administrative support and patient care. You should make note of who this person is, and introduce yourself if possible. There is often a large white board at the nurses' station that indicates the Charge Nurse (CNAs) for the current shift as well as which Registered Nurses (RNs) and Certified Nurse's Assistants are on the floor, and which patients are assigned to each. The Charge Nurse is one of the people I seek out when Mom is on the ward.

The Registered Nurses are next level of nurses and each carries a heavy load. Their responsibilities include physical exams and patient evaluation, medications including all medicine delivered by IV, wound care, catheter care, charting and transcribing doctors' orders and tracking patient progress. I have often heard nurses complain that they spend more time charting and doing paper work than what time they spend actually taking care of patients. I know they would rather be taking care of patients. The number of RNs on the floor will vary with the hospital census and staff availability. If you have an opportunity to choose which hospital you go to, it's a good idea to check on the nurse/patient ratio in that hospital. Nurses and CNAs run their butts off doing the best they can with the time they are on the floor. That said, it's often the case that staffing levels are cut by corporate hospital administrators to reduce costs, affecting nurses most. Most hospitals are businesses looking to make a profit, after all. Overloaded nurses are hard to catch up with sometimes, and are in and out of a patient's room quickly so they can get on to the next room. If Mom's nurse is nowhere to be found, I will go to the nurse's station and ask to speak to the Charge Nurse when she is available.

The staff members that Mom and most patients will see most are the CNAs. They have the most direct interaction with the patients, as they take vitals every hour on their shift along with all the other jobs they do. They assist patients with personal care, such as toileting, bathing, teeth brushing and feeding, if the patient needs assistance with these tasks. They will also be responsible for taking care of housekeeping tasks, such as changing beds and removing soiled gowns and linens. The CNA can be counted on to help the patient reposition him or herself in bed to be more comfortable, and avoid bed sores. The CNAs provide personal interaction and someone to talk to, which is especially important. The hospital can be a lonely place, even if there are many people moving around and making noise constantly. If family and friends can't be there to fill all the hours, the CNAs may be a real treasure.

Other hospital staff on the floor will include lab techs who move in and out as needed, and dietary staff, who will be those delivering meals and picking up empty trays. There will be physical therapists, occupational therapists, and social workers, each with their own focus on the patient, and each with their own set of "orders" from the doctor. Expect that these therapies and support professionals may seem to be less than perfectly coordinated, for example in the timing of visits, or consistency of direction. A little patience goes a long way, and asking clarifying questions, in a respectful way, is appreciated by everyone and sometimes as necessary as double-checking the medications list.

WHO IS THE ATTENDING PHYSICIAN TODAY?

Speaking of orders, where is the doctor in all this? In the old days, Mom's primary care physician (PCP) would come in to the hospital for "rounds." When I was taking care of my husband's parents back in the late 1990s, their doctor would make rounds every morning before he started seeing patients in his office at nine o'clock. I could arrive at the hospital around seven in the morning, and be pretty sure he would visit my mother-in-law by the time I had to leave for work at eight-thirty. It doesn't work that way anymore. About a decade ago, insurance companies began discouraging hospital visits from the PCP, in preference to doctors that were specifically trained to perform inpatient care, known as the hospitalist

A 2011 research study by two University of Texas Medical Branch geriatric internal medicine physicians, Drs. Kuo and Goodwin, examined the effect of the hospitalist model on hospital costs and on medical utilization and costs after a patient is discharged – as compared to costs when care is directed by a patient's PCP. It compared the costs to Medicare of five percent of all enrollees from 2001 to 2006, to determine how effective the hospitalist model was proving to be. The results showed that hospitalist care resulted in a shorter hospital stay (about half a day), and a total savings of fifty Medicare dollars on every hospitalization. What the study also found, was that those elderly patients treated by the hospitalist, with whom they have no personal relationship or history as they do with their PCP, were less likely to be released to home and instead more likely to be released to nursing facilities for further care. These patients were also more likely to return to the emergency room within thirty days of discharge. It turned out that the cost savings of the hospitalist per stay was actually offset by increased costs in the thirty days after discharge, with additional nursing home charges and more emergency visits. Not what I would call a good outcome for the patient or costs.

Although I am personally not a fan of the hospitalist movement, as caregivers, patients, or consumers of medical services, we don't have actual choices in the way that hospitals choose to run their businesses. This makes it our job, as caregivers and concerned family members, to work within the system to get the best possible care for those we love when they are in the hospital. It is the hospitalist that will review tests, medications and progress to determine what is the appropriate treatment for your loved one. The advantages of working with a hospitalist are that they are always in the hospital, and can respond to a crisis or inquiries from nurses on the floor quickly. This allows for more efficient execution of physician orders, and prompter answers to nurses' concerns and questions. It does not often allow for any time for the hospitalist to get to know a patient, or thoroughly review each patient's chart and medical history. I've had some of these practitioners ask some pretty silly questions, ones that made it clear they hadn't reviewed much before walking in the door. If you happen to be present when they show up, never be afraid to speak up if they are misinformed or uninformed about specific facts you can provide. Because they don't really know the patient, they don't talk to them much which impedes communication, leaves a patient feeling less confident in their care, and often hesitant to speak up. The hospitalist is more likely to look at clinical information, and use data and observations to direct care.

Hospitalists can make their daily visit with patients at any time during the day, because they work in the building, not primarily at an office off campus. This makes it very difficult to know when they will be there to see your loved one. You can inquire of the nursing staff as to when the doctor usually makes his visit to their ward, but in a hospital, there is no time frame that is cast in stone. Circumstances such as patient care emergencies and staffing rotations have a lot of influence, and doctors are expected to be flexible, too. Although the in-person interaction may be hit and miss, here's nothing wrong with leaving a message and asking them to call you with updates. The nurses can help with this. Some hospitalists are more willing to actually call you, the family member, themselves than others. I've actually have had the best luck getting updates by skipping chats with the elusive doctor, and talking to the nurses directly to find out what orders were left during the hospitalist's last visit, whenever that took place.

Another way to share information is to contact Mom's primary physician, and ask them for an update from the hospitalist. Communication between the doctor at the hospital and the PCP is also correlated to the best long-term positive outcomes for patients that have been hospitalized. If the hospitalist has not yet updated Mom's doctor when you call, it gives them a push to make a call and find out what is going on with their patient. Doctor-to-doctor communication is crucial, and often very complete. Moreover, the primary physician will be able to put the current ailment in complete context, and feel more sense of responsibility for Mom's total well being, beyond the immediate condition causing the hospitalization. Leave your message with the receptionist, and ask when you might expect a return call. If you don't get it before the end of the day, call back.

VISITING HOURS ARE JUST A SUGGESTION DO YOU REALLY HAVE TO LEAVE?

Once your loved one is settled into their bed, their meals are arranged, the nurse has all the information she needs, the lab people have been in and taken whatever fluid they need to test, it's time to rest. Resting in a hospital is hard to do, with all the outside noise and workers in and out of the room constantly. Hospitals have stated rules for visiting hours to manage the number of people in a room, and to allow the patient to rest. Some hospitals have specific visiting hours for different departments, while others require ID badges for all visitors. Find out what the rules are at your hospital.

Rules are sometimes rather flexible. Some hospitals will let you stay with your loved one if they are critically ill, and even set up a cot for you. Sometimes you just have to doze in the chair, which is what we did with my Dad until we got him moved to the hospital in Spokane where they had staff that could act as a "sitter" overnight to watch over him closely, so that family members could actually get some sleep. It was one of the only ways to get Mom to leave Dad's side.

It's a delicate balance knowing when to stay and when to go home. For me, part of the balance has to do with guilt about how to divide my time between tending to Mom in the hospital and keeping up with my husband, home and business clients' needs. Who gets what piece of the pie in the 24 hours in my day? How am I supposed to do it all and take care of myself, too?

Two of my best friends are nurses, and have told me that the best thing one can do for a loved one in the hospital is to be there with them as much as possible. I totally agree with that, but at the same time, the "as much as possible" part has to take into consideration self-care for the caregiver and the needs of her family. You can't take care of someone well if you don't take care of yourself. I have to admit that sometimes, I've not been very good at this. (I've heard lots of us are like that.) Lucky for me, I have a husband who loves me and watches out for me too, and knows to make sure I eat and rest. That's a good thing. Even so, there are times when he gets his nose a bit out of joint when he ends up with a smaller piece of the pie than he would prefer for a few days in a row. I can't blame him, but I can't really do much to change it either. All we can do is the best we can, and leave the rest up to the Universe.

For the long term, a real saving grace is to gather a core group of supporters that can take turns spending time with an elder while they're in the hospital. This is a priceless resource worth cultivating. In addition to family that are close by, don't forget to check with some friends and neighbors your elder may be close to, or with their church or other group like the VFW or a quilting circle. Visiting with these people will be good for their spirits and their health. If your supporters can take informal "shifts" that free you up for family, work and self-care, it becomes much easier to manage your own stress and guilt level for not being there all the time. Remember, there are only so many pieces of pie (your time and energy), and you can't always do it all, even if you think you should. Eventually you will burn out and trust me, it's not pretty.

Unless you are standing at death watch or another intensely critical situation, it's best to keep visitors to a small number, such as two at a time, and be very respectful of other patients in terms of noise level. If you have a large group of friends or family that have come to the hospital, rotating yourselves between the waiting room or cafeteria, and about two visitors with the patient at a time is the best way to go.

MOM'S GETTING BETTER - SHE'S CRANKY

When my Mom is first admitted, I generally know she will be there at least a couple of days. Based on Medicare rules, it will be at least two midnights if she is officially admitted. After those days, it certainly varies based on how she is responding to treatment. During those first days, there is no question that she is where she needs to be. She is fading in and out of sleep most of the time. Once she gets the right medicines, and the effects start to kick in, she begins showing signs of improvement and begins to perk up. I know she's better when she starts complaining about the food, how many times they woke her up, and asks when can she get the hell out of here?

CHAPTER FOUR:
DISCHARGE FROM THE HOSPITAL

Getting out of the hospital is a lot like resigning from a book club. You're not out of it until the computer says you're out of it.
~ Erma Bombeck

By the time this part of the process comes around, several days have passed and hopefully your loved one is making progress toward recovering from whatever brought them to the hospital in the first place. Most likely, you are exhausted, stressed and constantly adding to the list of things you haven't been able to do since you began this episode as a caregiver with a loved one in the hospital. You may hear a rumor that discharge is being considered. What do you do now? That's a really big question with multiple choice answers.

According to cms.gov, discharge planning involves:

Determining the appropriate post-hospital discharge destination for a patient;

- Identifying what the patient requires for a smooth and safe transition from the acute care hospital/post-acute care facility to his or her discharge destination; and
- Beginning the process of meeting the patient's identified post-discharge needs.
- Considerations for a patient's discharge ideally begins shortly after admission. Social Services will be advised as soon as your loved one is admitted. They are responsible for discharge planning.

Here are some key people to talk to prior to discharge and key questions to have answered before leaving the hospital. Communication with all the parts of the process is the best way to manage a successful hospital discharge.

Key People:
Hospital Discharge Planner / Social Services
- Primary Care Physician and Hospitalist
- Charge Nurse on Ward

Key Questions:
Is Mom ready to be discharged?
- Where will she go?
- What should we expect regarding recovery?
- Who do you call with questions and follow-up?
- What are all these pills for?

DISCHARGE TODAY - REALLY?

I found out the hard way how important it is to get in on the planning part as soon as possible. My first experience with a discharge plan gone wrong was with my father-in-law, early in my unplanned career as family caregiver. He had been in the hospital after a bout with the flu and a vitamin B deficiency, from not eating much for several days, which made him all but crazy for awhile. After a couple of days in the hospital, getting some antibiotics and vitamin supplements in him, he was feeling better and called my mother-in-law from his hospital room to say, "I'm at the bus station. Could you come pick me up?" That might have been okay if he hadn't been at the hospital and if Mom actually drove a car, but he wasn't and she didn't.

The next morning, I got a call at work from the discharge planner. She said, "Mr. McDaniels is being discharged this afternoon. Will you be picking him up?" Where is the plan in this scenario? It was the first I had heard about him being sent home, and based on the call the night before, I didn't see any way he could go home to his ninety year old wife who needed two insulin shots every day for her diabetes (she was used to having her husband give her the shots) in addition to multiple other medications for her heart disease. I had been taking care of these duties before and after work since Dad went into the hospital.

DISCHARGE TO WHERE?

I left work, and went to the hospital to find out what was going on and try to figure out what I was going to do. When I arrived at the nurses' station looking like a deer in the headlights, the charge nurse came to my rescue. I explained my dilemma to her, and she suggested a residential care home where her father currently lived. Looking back, I know there must have been guardian angels watching my back. I called the suggested facility, and went for a visit that day.

I did finally make contact with the discharge planner from social services. She had a list of resources for me to review, along with lots of other papers that really didn't seem to do me much good at the time. The instructions included, as they should, details for following up with Dad's regular doctor, the medications he was supposed to be taking, and symptoms to look out for that would indicate a relapse. Lesson learned, make these contacts early.

It was quite surreal going through the motions of collecting my father-in-law's personal clothing and such, packing them into a suitcase and some boxes, and collecting him at the hospital. I drove him to the residential care home, and took him to his room, while doing the best I could to explain to him why he couldn't go home. It broke my heart to leave him there.

You might wonder where my husband was during all this drama with his father and mother. The long and short of it is that he was at work 35 miles away in Spokane, making sure all of us had what we needed to take care of each other.

We had been in contact all day on the phone, so he knew what was happening. My in-town location allowed me the freedom to respond to parent care and feeding. That was how our care plan worked.

We'd been making dinner for the two of them twice a week for a year, to make sure they were eating well and to do "eyes on" visits at least twice weekly. We had known for a long time that they were at the end of their capabilities to safely care for each other, the house, and the idyllic lakeside property they lived on for nearly fifty years. Being a couple of stubborn old survivors of the depression from Oklahoma, they would have no part of our previous suggestions to move to somewhere where they could get help. Their attitude is most certainly not uncommon. No one wants to admit they are incapable of taking care of themselves, or their environment. My in-laws were no different. It often takes a crisis to push the envelope enough that changes can be made. Sometimes, hospital visits can be a way to initiate a transition from home to a different care environment. The discharge planner can be a great resource to you, if you take the time to explain what the realistic situation at home looks like for your loved one.

In the end, it was true that my father-in-law was medically improved enough to leave the hospital. Hospitals are intended for acute care only. Dad's mental state and living situation weren't considered as part of the picture. At the time, I didn't know that I could have challenged the discharge. I should have directly contacted Dad's primary care doctor, and the assigned social services representative, to voice my concerns and delay the discharge until we could arrange for a safer discharge. A discharge can be considered unsafe if someone is being sent home alone, or into a situation without adequate care due to lack of family resources or into the care of a spouse that has significant medical issues him- or herself.

In today's health care environment, it would have been more likely that Dad would have been discharged to a skilled nursing facility to receive rehabilitation, including physical therapy to improve his strength and balance to avoid falls, occupational therapy to assure he can do things like make himself a grilled cheese sandwich safely, or having balance to take out the trash. I'll share more about this rehab process in a skilled nursing facility in the next chapter.

GET REAL - HOW SAFE IS HOME

When the doctor, probably the hospitalist, decides that discharge is appropriate, the wheels start turning to open up a bed for someone else. Each hospital will have its own protocol for discharge, and as a caregiver you need to be involved from the start. If the decision has been made to release your loved one to home, take a good hard look at what needs to be done medically after their hospital stay.

- Do they have dressings that need to be changed?
- Are there restrictions on what they should eat?
- How often do they need to take medication and how likely they are to remember.
- Are there restrictions on lifting and moving?

Be brutally honest with yourself about your own situation and what availability, willingness and desire you have to do things like changing dressing and irrigating drainage tubes. There are lots of resources to help with these tasks. Your discharge planner should have a list of them for you. As long as the care is directed by an order from the patient's physician, care performed by a home health nurse is covered by Medicare. Here is a link to a Medicare PDF that gives the specific eligibility requirements for Medicare coverage for in home nursing care as well as advice in choosing an agency - Medicare Home Health.

My mother and I have a great relationship with her home healthcare nurses. When she was in her own home, I could call them any time of day, if necessary, to ask questions or make arrangements for them to make a home visit. She is now in an assisted living facility, and they still visit her there. I don't know what I would have done without them.

As a caregiver, you'll also have to be very frank about how much time you can spend helping your loved one with non medical things, like housekeeping, groceries, bill paying, doctor's visits, ad infinitum. If you already have a busy life with a job, husband, kids and friends that give you joy how much of that are you ready to let go of entirely? When you start seeing signs that a loved one's health is failing, that is the time to start thinking about what you can handle and maintain your own sanity. **You cannot take care of everyone else unless you take care of yourself first.**

DISCHARGE GONE RIGHT

There are, of course, situations where discharge is appropriate and desired. My mother has made multiple visits to the hospital in the last ten years, and we have had good discharge planning experiences. Discharge planning should be a team effort. When things go right, you know what to expect and the following items are considered and discussed with you and your loved one so everyone knows the game plan (from caregiver.org):

- ***Evaluation*** of the patient by qualified personnel
- ***Discussion*** with the patient or his representative
- ***Planning*** for homecoming or transfer to another care facility
- ***Determining*** if caregiver training or other support is needed
- ***Referrals*** to home care agency and/or appropriate support organizations in the community
- ***Arranging*** for follow-up appointments or tests.

If you find yourself and your loved one mid-way through a discharge day and don't have these considerations addressed, find someone who can address them. Contact your discharge planner or her supervisor.

GET THE MED LIST - CHECK IT TWICE

One of the key items to check on when leaving the hospital, regardless of where your loved one is being discharged to, is the medication list. Review the list you started with, and compare it to the list you get at discharge. Ask about changes and additions so you know why medications are being prescribed. If there are meds missing from your list at admission, find out why they have been discontinued. The American Society of Hospital Pharmacists offer some facts and statistics that demonstrate how often medication mistakes happen:

- Inadequate medication reconciliation accounts for 46% of all medication errors, with 20% of those resulting in harm.
- Seniors are at increased risk for medication related problems (MRPs) especially during transitions of care.
- Discrepancies in medication documentation are associated with increased 30-day re-hospitalizations.
- National 30-day Medicare hospital readmission rate is 19.1%.
- If you have questions about your loved one's medications, ask to speak to the hospital

pharmacist. They understand that you may know much more about how your loved one handles different medications than they do. If you have a question, ask your loved one's primary nurse or the charge nurse to initiate a contact with the pharmacist. Take advantage of this resource, during the hospitalization and especially at discharge.

YOUR LOCAL PHARMACIST IS YOUR FRIEND

I have been working with the same pharmacy tech at my local Safeway store since I began this journey with my in-laws many years ago, as well as pharmacists that have been on staff there for several years. They have always been my allies, and over the years have become welcome family friends who help me with so many things. The pharmacy tech is the face you see at the counter, and often the one you speak to on the phone when you call to renew a prescription. She's usually the one who knows what's going on with special orders and whether there is stock on hand. She masters the computer that tells her if your medicine is covered, and if the current prescription has expired. She's probably also the one who faxes or calls a provider to clarify what specific information needs to be on a prescription to have it covered by insurance. Get to know the pharmacy tech wherever you go.

The pharmacist's job is varied and vitally important. I am a bit partial, as my sister has her degree in pharmacy, and having a family pharmacist is a big bonus. Every time Mom's medication is changed, she's the one I call first. If I didn't have a sister to call, I would call my local pharmacists who I know and trust.

According to pharmacyregulation.org the following are general responsibilities of a pharmacist:

- Ensuring quality of medicines supplied to patients.
- Ensuring that the supply of medicines is within the law.
- Ensuring that the medicines prescribed to patients are suitable.
- Advising patients about medicines, including how to take them, what reactions may occur, and answering patients' questions.

Pharmacists also:

- Supervise the medicines supply chain, and ensure pharmacy premises and systems are fit for purpose.
- Advise other healthcare professionals about safe and effective medicine use, and safe and secure supply of medicines.
- Respond to patients' symptoms and advise on medicines for sale in pharmacies.
- Provide services to patients, such as smoking cessation, blood pressure measurement and cholesterol management.

- Supervise the production and preparation of medicines, and assess the quality of medicines before they are supplied to patients from pharmaceutical manufacturers.

I asked my local pharmacy staff for insight to the most common mistakes made when someone is discharged from the hospital. Their answer did not surprise me. The most common mistake is in reconciling old and new medication lists that include all meds taken before a medical crisis, what meds are added while in care, whether it is from emergency room care, hospital admission or changes at a nursing facility, and which ones have been discontinued.

If you find yourself navigating a discharge with your loved one, you will receive a list of medications as a part of your exiting paperwork. Take this list to your pharmacist, along with an accurate list of what was being taken before, or even a bag full of all the prescription bottles you find in your family member's cabinets, and they will help you get it straight. Please call ahead and make arrangements for this, so the pharmacist can schedule the time to spend with you. Most people, especially the elderly when they have had multiple ailments to recover from, have old and expired prescriptions in their medicine cabinet. You can separate the old ones out, and let the pharmacy dispose of them for you.

What you will gain from this process is a good clean list of medications you can maintain as the situation changes. The best way to manage a loved one's medication list is to have one that includes the drug name, strength, directions for use, and what ailment is being treated. Keep an accurate copy with your loved one, and keep one for yourself.

Another service that many pharmacies offer is bubble packaging, or filling medi-sets. These are very convenient, and will save you hours of our valuable time if you're the one responsible for filling up those pill boxes. This also takes away the anxiety of wondering if you did them all correctly, especially if you're dealing with more than five or so bottles of pills.

My pharmacist suggested that if your loved one is resistant to having you set up their pill box, have bubble packs or medi-sets done at the pharmacy instead. That way, Mom feels more independent about managing her medications, and you feel better for knowing all of her meds are included at the right times. This is also a good way to find out if they are not taking meds they should be. Sometimes doctors will prescribe new medications for an ailment that is not improving, when the reality is that the patient is not taking the medication already prescribed. This can also happen when patients don't have enough money to buy prescriptions and groceries. When asked what was the most helpful thing a caregiver could do for their loved one as it relates to the medications they need to take, they told me it was to be present at all doctor visits, so you hear things first hand. Always have your medication list with you at these visits so you can keep up with changes. One of my bonus offers for readers of this book is a blank form you can use to create your own medication list. You will find it at jackiemcdaniels.com.

Figuring out who will pay for medications is a whole other story of complexity and confusion. All insurance companies have specific lists of drugs that are covered under their plan. These are called "formularies." Your loved one's insurance company probably sends you a formulary list each new coverage year. I am guessing most people just file it away or round file it, but it contains important information. Check out medications your loved one is taking, to make sure they are on the list of covered drugs. If not, you may need to get prior authorization to have that medication or service covered. This means that you must have your loved one's doctor write a letter to the insurance company explaining why they need a medication that is not on the current formulary. They have the choice to authorize coverage or not. It is up to you to follow up with the doctor, and the insurance company, to make this happen. Your pharmacy may be able to help you with this, so don't be afraid to ask questions.

Getting refills on prescriptions is another issue that caregivers deal with, and the helpful hint I received from my favorite pharmacy technician is to never let prescriptions run out before ordering your refills. When you have about five days left, it is a good time to order. This gives plenty of time for refills to be approved if a prescription has expired. Most doctors require twenty-four to forty-eight hours to respond to refill requests. Giving yourself five days or so will allow plenty of time for faxes and phone calls to go back and forth to get things approved. There is no reason to put yourself in a panic because the pills are all gone and you can't get anymore until Tuesday. Make sure you also mark dates in your calendar for prescription duration and refill dates, and confirm the schedule and supply you will have on discharge from the hospital.

YOU'RE FINALLY OUT OF THE HOSPITAL - NOW WHAT???

After jumping through potentially many hoops, medically and procedurally speaking, your loved one has recovered enough to leave the hospital and the both of you are on your way to the next step of recuperation. It is such a relief to have them well enough to leave, but in many ways this is a double-edged sword, because you must now devote efforts to making sure your loved one is properly cared for going forward. Sometimes we are not sure just what that looks like, or what it involves. Read on, and we'll explore some options.

CHAPTER FIVE:
AFTER THE HOSPITAL

MANY ROADS TO RECOVERY

"One's doing well if age improves even slightly one's capacity to hold on to that vital truism: This too shall pass."
~ *Alain de Botton*

The resilience of the human body and spirit amaze me. For all the years that I have been an intimate part of the lives of the elderly and guided them through all kinds of medical crises, I have been humbled by their ability to endure and recover from illness. So many times, I have sat at a bedside and wondered how these frail old bodies can possible come back from states of being that feel close to death. For each of those I sat with, they recovered and left the hospital, all but the last time.

When discharge orders are written, the main consideration should be what type of environment will be most beneficial to the recovery of the patient, and in what setting can ongoing care be best provided. This is a multiple choice question, and often a difficult one to answer with everyone's agreement. There are a variety of discharge options available when the round the clock care and resources of the hospital are no longer necessary. At the time of discharge, the progress of resolving whatever medical crisis brought you to the hospital will generally dictate the type of environment that is best.

LONG TERM CARE – WHAT TO PREPARE FOR

We've been lucky that my Mom hasn't had to be under skilled nursing care for more than two or three weeks at a time. These stays followed her bouts with urinary infections and out of control blood sugars. All too often, when elder loved ones suffer from things like hip fractures, stroke, or extended treatments for cancer, unfortunately the recovery period is delayed or uncertain. In these instances, some type of long-term care is necessary. My mother-in-law fell while simply walking to the bathroom, at the assisted living facility where she and my father-in-law were living, and broke her hip. She was ninety-four at the time. After undergoing surgery and spending a few days in the hospital, she was transferred to a skilled nursing home for recovery and rehabilitation. Her stay was expected to be about eight weeks. Somewhere around week six, she began a downward spiral marked by severe mental deterioration, and the return of congestive heart failure symptoms that had plagued her for several years. She never recovered, and my husband and I were by her side when she took her last breath.

This is not an unusual trajectory for the elderly with hip fractures. According to the American Academy of Orthopedic Surgeons, the 30-day mortality rates for seniors suffering from fractures ranges from 9 percent for a relatively healthy individual, to 17 percent if the patient already has an acute medical problem. If a patient has heart failure while being treated for a hip fracture, the 30-day mortality rate increases to 65 percent.

When a loved one is a resident in a skilled facility for an extended length of time, there should be care conferences involving the treatment team on a regular basis, to review progress and prognosis. Family caregivers should also be a part of this, and I attended several. It's the only opportunity to get a well-rounded view of the department management at the facility, and discuss their expectations and plans for treatment. If there are issues with your loved one's care, or the personnel caring for them, this is the time to surface those. The managers are not usually the ones to actually provide care, but the people who report to them must follow through with instructions they are given. Provide appropriate input, and then follow up with the feedback they need to make sure any issues are addressed.

The POLST (Physician's Order for Life Sustaining Treatment), a form that I introduced in the beginning, is especially important when your loved one is receiving long term care. Nursing homes and assisted living facilities need to have one of these forms on file for your family member. This form will be recognized by the paramedics if the facility must call them in a crisis, and they will in turn honor your loved ones wishes for end of life treatment.

If long term or custodial care is necessary, be sure to do your research. If you've been given enough lead time to investigate your options for a skilled nursing facility (SNF), you'd be well advised to visit them in person. There is nothing wrong with showing up unannounced before you decide on one. From my own experience, they can differ greatly from clean, quiet and friendly to dark, smelly and cold. Depending on where you live, you may not have a choice, as available beds may be few and far between. Sometimes you take what you can get, but knowing a bit about the facilities near you or your loved one allows you to make informed choices whenever options are available.

Don't be afraid to ask doctors, nurses or social workers you know, in the hospital setting, if they would have a preference for their mother if making a similar decision. Ask friends and relatives for referrals, if you know they have been in your shoes in the past. If you choose one that doesn't work out as you expected, don't beat yourself up for making the wrong choice. Learn from the experience, make a different choice next time, and let it go. Start shopping for an alternative. The website, A Place For Mom, has a large database of facilities all over the country and can even provide a list of facilities with current openings.

A close friend of mine had just moved to a new area, and was doing some internet searches to find a facility for her mother who has Alzheimer's, and needs to be in a secure setting. She entered her contact info at A Place For Mom, and within minutes she received a phone contact from them. Her first reaction was concern and a bit of irritation that she had potentially unleashed a constant marketing pest that would call her every night at dinner time. As it turned out, that was not the case. In fact, they have become a good resource for her and her mother.

NOT LONG TERM BUT NOT HOME - REHAB IN A SKILLED NURSING FACILITY

When Mom had her catheter placed, the urologist warned us that our greatest challenge would be avoiding urinary tract infection, commonly referred to as UTI. I was familiar with these, as my father-in-law had urinary issues for years. UTIs are very common in older patients, and have a wide range of symptoms beyond urinary discomfort, including fever, nausea and disorientation. These can look very different from UTI in a younger patient. When Mom developed her first UTI, she showed none of these symptoms. Instead, her blood sugar spiked to the 600-range, and she could barely stand, as she was so weak. The first time this happened, I took her to the emergency room. After a couple of hours of waiting for triage, lab work and all the other things you wait for in emergency, she was admitted for insulin infusion in the critical care unit to stabilize her blood sugars, with additional diagnoses of dehydration and a UTI. She transferred to a general medical unit one day later, and stayed there for four more days.

By the time she started greeting me with, "Get me out of here," she was much better, but also still on IV medications, and still very weak and unsteady. She may have been miserable in the hospital, but there was no way she could go home without constant care. She needed time to get her strength back, before she could be back at home on her own. Enter our first recommendation for a stay at a skilled nursing care center. Explaining to Mom that instead of leaving the hospital to go home, she was leaving it to go to a nursing home for "a while" was one of the most gut wrenching conversations I have had with her. Her parents each spent time in nursing homes, and I know it was a horror to her to think of herself in one. Yet I knew it was exactly what was needed, just like the doctor did.

Having been through this with my in-laws years before, I already knew which facilities I did *not* want Mom to go to. The skilled nursing facility we chose was near the hospital, and run by a local geriatric physician. Transport was provided, and I followed behind. A nurse greeted us warmly, checked us in, and went over Mom's discharge paperwork with me. In many ways, the process is very similar to hospital admittance. We verified all her medications, including new ones added while she was in the hospital. A thorough skin exam followed, to note whether she was developing any bed sores or skin issues the staff needed to monitor. These are especially common in patients who are bedridden and seldom move around. I was comfortable that they could take care of Mom until she could come home.

I remember distinctly how I felt, that very first time in the nursing home, as I got Mom settled into her bed and put the flowers we brought from her hospital room onto the window ledge. I so hated to leave her there, even though I knew it was the right thing to do. I felt sad, and unable to ward off the guilt monster in my head, intently reminding me how many times Mom had told me she didn't want to be in a nursing home.

Thankfully, Mom also knew she was too weak to be on her own, and understood the necessity of the nursing home stay. The lesson I've learned about guilt over the years: when I'm already doing the best I can to help Mom through her medical crisis of the moment, that's all I can do — my best. Wishing things were otherwise is a waste of time and energy that is better invested in helping her to recover, regain her strength and health to whatever degree possible, and be thankful to have her here with me still.

THE LONG DAYS THAT FOLLOW ADMISSION

In the skilled nursing environment, whether in long term care or short-term rehab, patients are expected to get up and dressed each day, if they are able. Residents need to bring loose, comfortable clothes that allow free movement while exercising, and good non-skid shoes. Also bring nightgowns, a robe, non-skid slippers, and a jacket for outdoors. As long as they are able, patients are generally encouraged to spend time outside. If they receive physical therapy, the therapists may also walk with the patient outside of the building, to evaluate how they walk on uneven ground and deal with curbs and obstacles. All the items you bring in must be labeled, even if you will be doing their laundry. I would suggest that for as long as it's practical, family caregivers would do well to handle their loved one's laundry. Things get lost, or come back damaged or badly faded, and we've ended up with several items that didn't belong to us. As in the hospital, it's best to leave valuables at home.

If your loved one likes word puzzles or books, they will enjoy having something to help pass the time. For my mother, as well as others, time moves very, very slowly while she is a resident in this kind of facility. She looks forward to her physical therapy time, because it gives her something else to do. In her case, she has been more highly functional than many of the other long-term residents her age, which makes her feel out of place and at a loss for what to do with herself. Talk to the staff, find out what kinds of activities they provide, and encourage your loved one to attend. If you can, make contact with the activities coordinator, and talk to them about the kinds of things your loved one likes to do. Activities help a lot to break up the day, and relieve boredom. So many times, elders in skilled facilities are essentially waiting simply waiting for the day to end, or waiting for you to come for a visit. Quite often there is musical entertainment, bingo, crafts, or other activities that can help pass the time, if your loved one is willing to give them a try. My mother isn't very outgoing, so she has to be pushed a bit to become involved in social situations. She usually has a good time, once she decides to go.

Having a loved one in a skilled facility is also much like having them in the hospital, in that being involved in their care is a key part of maintaining continuity in medications and treatment. I make a point of conversing with Mom's assigned nurses, or the nurse manager, to introduce myself. In the process, I can find out when the facility doctor might see her, and what their plan for her continued care looks like. It often takes them a day or so to create and initiate that plan. The staff will need to coordinate physical therapy, occupational therapy, a bathing schedule, and meal requirements. Be patient, but be persistent.

The first few days I may visit daily, but once Mom starts getting used to the routine, I skip a day or two in between visits, make a point to talk to her on the phone, and connect with the nurses if either of us have questions or concerns. Just like in the hospital, find out when shift changes happen, because this is a bad time to call to check up on your loved one. When the shift changes, the nurses meet and exchange notes on patients, so that one shift knows what the other shift did, what developed during the course of the day, and what still needs to happen. Ask what the best times to call would be, and save yourself the frustration of calling when there is no one available to talk to you.

Becoming familiar with the staff and getting to know the people who will actually be treating your loved one is vital. Nurses and CNAs are usually so stretched with the responsibilities of their patients that getting their attention for even a minute, as they go hustling from one patient room to the other is often difficult at best. If yours is a familiar face that they come to associate with positive encounters that are friendly, respectful of their time, and appreciative you will have a much easier time getting their attention to address whatever questions you may have. If you have questions, always speak up. If there is no one seen working near your loved one's room, go to the nurse's station, and hang around until someone talks to you.

Another challenge in the nursing home could be the roommate. Most of the time, rooms will be semi-private. That means dealing with another person's idiosyncrasies and ailments. Some people want the TV on all the time, sometimes loudly. Some people cry out in the night. Some people want lights on, some want them off. Be prepared, have patience and ask to be moved if there is a real incompatibility. Beds are not always available, but it never hurts to ask.

GETTING IN IS EASIER THAN GETTING OUT

My mother has been in the same nursing facility for a rehab stay several times, over the past three years, and by the time she leaves, she is physically ready to do most things for herself again. Most often, her stays have been about fourteen days in length. Somewhere around day ten, she begins reciting that old refrain, "Get me out of here!"

The first time she was in the nursing home, I pretty well agreed that she was well enough to come home by day ten. I went to social services, and asked when discharge was planned, and what I needed to do to have her released to go home. I think it was a Wednesday, and I wanted to have her home before the weekend. Most doctors aren't in the office on weekends, and getting discharge orders then is unlikely. What I learned from that first experience, was that it generally takes about three days to get out of one of these places. Forms and reports must be coordinated between social services and each department in the nursing home, such as physical/occupational therapy, the managing doctor at the facility, and the primary care doctor the patient usually sees. Doctor's orders have to be written before this process can even begin. Faxes have to be sent from one place to the other, and protocols must be followed. I can't adequately explain how frustrated I was, when I found out how many steps and how many days of persistence it took to get Mom discharged.

With that lesson learned, I started inquiring about discharge about day eight or nine, depending on Mom's progress, because I know it will take three days to get her sprung. The courses of medicines she takes usually last fourteen days, and I plan ahead from the day they begin treatment. Every situation is different, just as every medical emergency and its resolution is different. Family caregiver involvement can really help manage the process, leading to the best outcomes for their loved ones, and shortest stays in nursing home care.

ASSISTED LIVING – SAFER THAN HOME ALONE

Unfortunately, at some point going home may not be a real option anymore. Caregivers will come to the realization that home is no longer a safe place for their loved one to recuperate, or that their condition has deteriorated to where independent living is no longer practical. Our family put it off for a long time, but Mom's continued trips to ER, hospital stays and midnight calls for me to come over and help her because she didn't know what to do to help herself became too much for me to handle, and made me fearful for her being alone.

An incident unrelated to health scared me just as badly. I got a phone call from her one day, asking me what company she had her cable service with, and what she pays for the service. When I asked why she was asking, she calmly told me that a man had come to the door with a really good deal for cable service, and she couldn't find her last bill to tell him what she was already paying. As I told her she didn't need new cable service, she started talking to the "nice young man" that she had already let in the house and was still standing there while she was going through her bills and private papers. OMG! I immediately told her to ask him to leave, and we would discuss it later. When I saw her later that day, I explained that I was upset because he could have been an axe murderer. She just said, "Well, I didn't think of that." She promised me she wouldn't let anyone else in the house, but I wasn't convinced.

A few months later, I called a family meeting. My siblings came from their respective homes in other states, so we could explain to Mom that as much as she wanted to remain in her home, she wasn't safe there anymore. To help make the transition easier, we told her that if she stayed at an assisted living apartment for the winter but was physically better by spring, she could come back to the house. We didn't really think she would be able to come back, but it made the decision seem not so final. This is such a hard decision to make, but often the right one.

There are many options with choosing an assisted living facility, or as they are called in some states, adult foster care. Choose the environment that is best for your loved one. If he or she is active and engaged, consider a larger facility with community activities and field trips. My mother loves to garden, so I found a place where she could do this. She doesn't socialize all that well, so the forty resident complex where she lives now is much better than the sixty-five resident complex where she moved to at first. Just like investigating skilled nursing facilities, ask for referrals and do your research in advance. Make an appointment to tour a prospective place, and even have lunch. If you do not care to eat the food, your loved one probably won't either.

Sometimes, even though you've thoroughly checked out a facility and are sure it's the right one, after a few weeks or a few months, the place you chose just doesn't work out. I chose the wrong place the first time around, and I know others who have had to try a couple of places before finding the right combination of environment and care. Don't be afraid to be the squeaky wheel if you are not happy with the care being provided. Talk to the facility manager and the managing nurse. If things don't change, start shopping. Our home health nurse was the one who suggested the place my mother lives in now. When I told other providers where she was moving to, I got very positive responses. So far, our second time's a charm. Keep trying until you find what works for you. There are many options available these days, from large complexes to private homes in residential settings.

THERE'S NO PLACE LIKE HOME

Anyone leaving the hospital after a medical emergency wants to go home to familiar environs and comforts. Sometimes home is the best place for a loved one to continue their recovery, but family caregivers need to consider the whole picture: the loved one's abilities, both physical and mental, the continued treatment needed, and honestly evaluate who is the best person to provide the assistance needed. Caregivers also need to be honest with themselves and with other family members about how much time and responsibility they can commit to care, without completely disrupting life at home and their own family needs, plus work and self care, which is often harder in practice than you might think. As much as you may want to, or feel the obligation to care for a loved one returning from the hospital, you must be truly honest with yourself about what you can realistically do on a routine basis.

Can you really deal with changing bloody dressings? Can you flush a drainage tube? Are you able to safely assist your 200-pound father from his bed, and steady him on the way to the bathroom? Sometimes, elders are less comfortable receiving personal hygiene or bathing assistance from their children, especially those of the opposite sex. How many days in a row can you really devote hours, before and after work, to preparing meals and giving medication? Does your loved one truly understand the instructions they were given regarding limitations on diet, weight bearing or lifting? Not understanding or remembering instructions can lead to complications. Consider these things before you sign up for more than you are truly prepared or able to give, and consider ways to get your loved one the help they need that makes the most of everyone's resources, dignity, and experience.

My first experience testing this balance came about after an outpatient surgery my mother had a few years ago. She had been fighting a staph infection in a rather large wound on her shin, sustained in falling off of a wooden box (that she shouldn't have been standing on) while changing a light bulb. Her body reacted badly to the antibiotics she had to take, and she'd been feeling yucky and fighting antibiotic-induced diarrhea for days. I made my daily call to check in on her and instead of the usual, "Hi there. How's Mom today?" I said, "Hi Mom. What's new in your world today?" Her answer was not what I expected. She said, "You know, I don't think I've peed in a couple of days."

Really? She didn't think it was important to report this earlier, maybe even yesterday? If I asked her, she would say she didn't want to bother me. Bless her heart, she tries so hard to hang on to her independence. I have no doubt, when my time comes, I will be somewhat similar about wanting to do things for myself. Needless to say, we made a trip to the emergency room, and within a few days we saw a urologist. At the age of eighty-two, my mother's bladder essentially decided to give up the ghost. The combination of her age, four children and thirty years of being diabetic had caused enough nerve and muscle damage that a catheter was the only answer. We made arrangements to have a permanent supra-pubic catheter placed.

The surgery went well, and took only an hour and a half, in the door to out. I stayed with Mom for the first full day, and made arrangements for home health nurses to perform wound care and check up on her for the next several days. They also worked with both of us to show us how to change from her large nighttime urine bag, to the smaller leg bag she would wear during the day. This was a bit more of a challenge than normal, due to Mom's limited vision, but she was getting it figured out. So far…so good.

A couple of days later, I got a call from Mom to say that she thought I should come over and see what was going on with her catheter. She wouldn't explain further, just reiterated that I needed to come over. When I arrived, I found her urine bag bright red with blood that shouldn't be there. It scared the hell out of me, and had frightened her as well. That time I called the paramedics, and had them transport her to the hospital. The cause of the bleeding was irritation to the interior of her bladder. When Mom was questioned, we learned that the source of the irritation was that she was trying to wrestle clean sheets onto her bed by herself, just two days after having a hole put in her abdomen.

What was she thinking? Well, she wasn't thinking. Your confidence that your loved one knows and understands what it means to rest, follow doctors' instructions and ask for help when they need it is an especially important consideration when they live alone. If they don't understand, they could endanger themselves and end up back in the hospital or worse.

WHERE DO YOU FIND THE HELP YOU NEED

Upon discharge from the hospital, social services often provides a list of outside resources you can investigate if you need to bring help into your loved one's home after a hospital visit. Included in the list will most likely be the Area Agency on Aging. This federal program was created by the Older Americans Act in 1965, and has been updated a number of times since. The program provides the states with grants to support the development of programs for older adults and their caregivers. It is a national network of 56 State agencies on aging, 629 area agencies on aging, nearly 20,000 service providers, 244 Tribal organizations, and 2 Native Hawaiian organizations representing 400 Tribes. Here is a link to the Eldercare Locator website to find services for your state: www.eldercare.gov. States use different entities to coordinate theses programs within each individual state. Eldercare Locator will get you to the proper agency for your state. These programs can be a lifeline for you and your loved one, and may allow them to remain at home just a little longer.

Over the years, each time Mom has gone through an inpatient stay and rehab, she hasn't quite made it back to the same level of health and strength as she went in with. After one of her hospital stays, I called several home health agencies that provide non-skilled services such as help with house cleaning, grocery shopping, doctor visits and companionship. I was mostly interested in securing help with housework, especially heavy tasks such as vacuuming and changing the bed linens. I was able to help her with other chores. I could have helped with the housework, too, but Mom drew the line at that herself, insisting she didn't want me cleaning her house when I was already doing everything else. I had to admit that she was right about this. It prompted me to evaluate all I was doing for her, and having someone else do these things was good for both of us. Besides, it would give her someone else to talk to.

I tried a couple of different agencies, yet I was not happy with the people they sent us. They were nice young women and pleasant to Mom, but they didn't seem to know how to clean a house. I was fortunate to get a personal referral from a friend for a kind and helpful woman to help us out. She has been working for us and helping Mom for several years now, and I don't know what I would do without her. Years earlier, we also found a companion and helper for my in-laws through a referral from their assisted living facility. Her relationship with our family has persisted to this day, long since both of my husband's parents have passed away. If you can find a good helper or agency to assist your loved one, it can take some of the pressure off of you, the caregiver, so you can focus on the tasks that only you can do.

Hiring someone to come into your loved one's home is difficult at best. In addition to finding someone that is competent at the tasks you need handled, you want someone that your loved one is comfortable with and even likes, as he or she will be working in the home. Finding someone who is a good fit with your loved one and your situation can be a huge challenge, but it can be done. You must also consider security. If you are using an agency, they should be doing background checks on their employees, certainly ask about this. If you are hiring someone privately, you will need do background checks yourself, and get referrals and references. Although we want to believe that people working with the elderly are honest and trustworthy, problems with theft, misuse of property, even abuse, occur all too often. Do your homework, and then continue to monitor the service provider's activities, interactions with your loved ones, and their assets. Trust is important, but it also must be earned.

CONCLUSION

"It is one of the most beautiful compensations of life, that no man can sincerely try to help another without helping himself."
~ Ralph Waldo Emerson

Not all caregivers are doing the job because they chose to. Sometimes, it just works out that way and it can be very scary if you don't feel confident about what you are supposed to do when a crisis arises. I hope the information and stories I've shared can help other caregivers understand how to deal with such emergencies with confidence so that the medical community can do their job of diagnosing and treating your loved one, and you as a family caregiver can focus on yours, by managing care and advocating for the best care possible.

As the oldest daughter in a family of two girls and two boys, I began my first practice as a caregiver with my siblings when I was growing up. I was Mom's built-in babysitter for years. Move the clock forward fifty years, and my Mom would tell you I am still her "go to girl" but I'm taking care of her, instead of my brothers and sister, that I still refer to as "the kids." As it turned out, I was fortunate to have this kind of experience early in life, as things seem to have come full circle to bring me to where I am today. I am still the family caregiver, but this time it is for my mother. Roles reverse, generations change, and we do what we must to care for each other. This is what we do as humans, especially as women, we nurture and cooperate to make each other's lives better.

Being a caregiver for an aging loved one can begin quite innocently, with providing a home cooked meal a couple of times a week, or some routine help with yard work, and morph into something much more complicated and stressful than some time in the kitchen and sharing a dinner table. I hope the information presented here will help both new and seasoned caregivers to feel more confident and prepared to manage the medical matters of their loved one, as well as finding ways to do so with limited frustration and confusion in spite of how the medical machine of our time functions.

Like Boy Scouts and Girl Scouts, caregivers need to "be prepared." If you have not already done so, be sure to have the critical information needed to help medical staff efficiently treat your loved one in a medical emergency by preparing a Vial of Life Kit that is available and complete with data such as past and present medical conditions, current medication information, allergy info, family and physician contact information. Take the time to prepare legal forms ahead of emergencies, especially the Medical Durable Power of Attorney and Advanced Directives. These forms give you the legal right to speak for your loved one if they cannot speak for themselves, and to incorporate their own choices for end of life treatment. It is ideal that you take some time one-on-one to work these out with your loved one, before a situation arises that puts both of you under duress.

When you get "The Call", keep calm and ask the right questions to make an initial evaluation to determine how serious the situation is and what action to take next. A trip to the emergency room is always stressful, but knowing what to expect makes it so much easier to deal with. Providing accurate information to nurses during triage sets the stage for how doctors proceed with diagnosis and treatment. Get to know your emergency nurse and rely on them to help you and your loved one through your crisis. Doctor's orders are the only documents that count when hospital staff is treating your loved one. When the emergency doctor sees your loved one, their assessment and orders will dictate what happens next. Ask as many questions as you can think of while the doctor is in the treatment room, they don't stay long.

When an admission is advised, follow your loved one from ER to the treatment floor so you can go through any intake done by nurses on the ward. Don't assume all the info you gave when you arrived in the emergency room will arrive intact. Reviewing medication lists is essential. If medications are missing, ask if they have been discontinued on purpose, or if there has been an inadvertent omission.

Being an advocate for a loved one in the hospital is truly essential to good medical care. Make every effort to remain involved in their daily treatment by either being there (which is best but not practical or possible all the time) or by maintaining consistent phone contact with treating nurses, nurse managers and physicians. Find out when shift changes occur, and what the best times to call will be. If you leave a message and don't receive a call back, make another call. In most cases, nurses really want to return calls in a timely fashion, but work at hand and patient needs will dictate the time they have available.

Discharging from the hospital can be a complicated process, and usually involves social services discharge planners. Evaluations and treatment plans must be submitted by multiple departments, and there are multiple considerations for what environment provides the best location for care and recovery based on your loved one's medical condition. Being discharged to home is always the best case and a desired outcome after a medical crisis, but is it really the best place for your loved one to recover? Can they get the help they will need, and will they accept that help? In their current condition, are they really safe at home? If they answer is yes, take advantage of the resources available and make this happen, it will be a source of peace and comfort.

Talk to the doctor about home health nurses, and what services they may be able to provide. If ordered by the doctor, these services are generally covered by Medicare, and include nursing, physical, speech and occupational therapies. Counseling services are also available to help your loved one with transitions, like accepting loss of their independent lifestyle due to illness, and coping with a body that is wearing out from decades of just living. Contact your local Area

Agency on Aging to find out what services they can direct you to, as well. You can find the managing agency for your state with the Eldercare Locator. Their services can range from adult day care, to caregiver respite programs, to practical help with decoding hospital bills and Medicare coverage and many services in between. Some of these services are free of charge, some are payable on income-based fee schedules, and some are subsidized through various government programs. This is a valuable resource that is there to help both an aging loved one and a family caregiver.

When going home is not an option upon discharge, skilled nursing facilities for long-term care or short-term rehabilitation may be the next stop after the hospital. Caregivers need to maintain the same kind of vigilance in this environment as they did in the hospital, and the path is smoothed somewhat by getting to know doctors, nurses, nurse's assistants, social services staff and case managers. Be present at care conferences, and be open and honest about your evaluation of the care being received. If it's not up to snuff, ask if things will change. Give them a fair opportunity, but make arrangements to move to another facility if you must. Once you expect your loved one to discharge from a skilled facility, plan ahead and expect it to take about three days to get all the paperwork where it needs to be, so your loved one can be sent home. Stay in close contact with the primary care doctor, and make sure they are getting regular updates of treatments and progress.

Caring for an aging loved one could be described much like the Peace Corps slogan, "The toughest job you will ever love." There is no doubt it's tough at times, but the work is fueled and endured by the power of love. Although I titled this book *Daughters on Duty*, I am completely aware that it's not just daughters that provide care and concern for elder parents. I know that caregivers come in both genders, a wide range of ages, and that there are millions of us who provide loving care to someone in need, whether as a family, friend or paid caregiver, and each of us has the ability to improve and enhance the life of someone making their way through the challenging home stretch of their lives.

If you have chosen to live in the same household as your loved one in order to care for them, I hope you know what a blessing that is for them, and most likely for you too, when you are not too exhausted to think about it. Even if your loved one does not live with you, as mine did not, it doesn't mean their care doesn't take a toll on your life and your peace if you're not careful, or that you should feel guilty that you cannot care for them in your own home. Every situation is different and loving care, in whatever form it takes, is a blessing for all. The old adage is true: you must put your own oxygen mask on first, before helping others. You can't take care of all the people in your life if you don't take care of yourself first, and don't forget to give yourself that pat on the back now and then that I know you so richly deserve.

Please also check out my website jackiemcdaniels.com for some free downloads and bonus materials just for readers, as my gift to you.

EPILOGUE

"Daughters on Duty" was originally written in 2014 while I was still managing my mother's care. It was a blessing to be able to share it with her before her passing in 2015. I remember her asking me if the hands displayed on the front cover were ours. I miss her every day.

When you've been caring for someone for a long time and their time here on earth comes to an end it's hard to know how to feel or what to do next. So much of your time and energy has been devoted to being a caregiver. It's easy to feel like you have forgotten who you were before "The Call" changed everything. From my own experience I would say give it time. I know, everyone says that but it's true. Give yourself some time to decompress and settle into your new situation, whatever it might be.

After a long period of managing care and watching the one you love decline, it often feels like a relief when they pass away. They are no longer struggling and in pain. For my mother, she had been missing my father for fifteen years and when she passed I could feel nothing but gratitude that they were finally together again. That is not to say that feelings of guilt didn't creep in because I was relieved. They did. The truth is the whole process is incredibly hard and different for every one of us. That said, we will all take our turn at leaving this world and we really have no control of when that will be.

What we can do is to approach these challenges with compassion for ourselves and the ones we love. I chose to make sure the photos I see of my lost loved ones were in the happy, healthy years. Those are the memories I want to have. Those are the memories that your loved ones would want you to hold in your heart when you think of them and the love you put into their care.

ACKNOWLEDGEMENTS

This piece of work would not have happened if it were not for the love, trust and support of my amazing husband, Mike McDaniels. He not only supported my decision to write this book, but has always been there for me, no matter what I challenge myself to do. We have traveled this caregiver road together. He is an inspiration to me every day.

Our family has been, and always will be, a source of strength and love. I am grateful to my siblings Mitch, John & Lori and their spouses, for all the moral support they provide, as my husband and I manage Mom's needs on the home front. I know you are always there if I need you.

Many thanks for all the help and input from my favorite pharmacy staff at my local Safeway store. Kelly, Beth & Marci provide stellar customer service, and their honest, caring approach, have made working with them a pleasure of many years. Your generous input to this book is so appreciated.

Mom and I would have been lost without the care and expertise of our Crest Home Health nurses. Many more seniors would be able to continue living at home longer if these services were available to them. Thanks so much to Jennifer, Tricia, and all the compassionate caregivers that have come to our rescue when called.

When living at home was no longer a safe place, finding the right place for Mom to live wasn't the easiest thing. The compassionate and positive staff at Legends Park Assisted Living has made Mom feel welcome, cared for and cared about from the first luncheon we shared there. It has been such a relief to me, as a caregiver, to feel confident that Mom is being taken care of, and meanwhile my participation in her care is encouraged and appreciated.

I would be remiss if I did not acknowledge my own heritage as a driving force in creating and completing this book. My maternal grandmother, Sara, a loving and patient teacher in some of the most challenging situations, such as not sharing a common language with her students, as well as her sister, the Sister, Mary Jean Dorcy, O. P., most certainly channeled their talents, love and sense of humor through me as I created this work that I know they would both be most pleased with. Know, that I have felt your presence as the words met the page.

The other contingent of my support system is my girlfriends, most of who are or have been caring for their mothers for the past several years. We all might have been "off our rockers crazy" had we not been able to share our respective stories of trauma, heartbreak, frustration and stress with each other and ease the pain of these things with the laughter and love that other daughters on duty can naturally provide.

Lastly to all the daughters on duty, whether you are a daughter or not, what you do is important and valuable beyond wealth. Thank you for all you do. The kindness and compassion that drives family caregivers constantly adds to the positive vibrations the Universe holds for all of us. If we can love and take care of each other, all *will* be well and as it should be.

ABOUT THE AUTHOR

Jackie's involvement in elder care began in the early nineties as a caregiver to her in-laws and later to her mother, after the sudden death of her father in 2000. The knowledge she shares comes not from a degree in nursing or social work but from her first hand experiences of spending countless hours in the hospital with her elder parents and learning how to navigate the often overwhelming environment of a hospital while watching over those she loves. She lives in beautiful north Idaho with her husband and their dog Sophie adopted from Humane Society.

Contact Info: Jackie McDaniels
212 W. Ironwood Dr. Ste. D #360
Coeur d'Alene, ID 83814
Website: www.jackiemcdaniels.com
Email: jackiemcd1952@gmail.com

MOM'S BLUE RIBBON CAKE: A POEM BY JACKIE MCDANIELS

When I was a little girl, blessed to be your daughter, you gave me the basics in life. This was the love and stability that was the flour, well sifted.

Our family grew and I became a sister. I learned about nurturing a sibling and embracing kinship, this was the sugar that sweetens living.

Your encouragement and support in my school years added the baking soda, so I could rise to my full potential. You also showed me the value of hard work and perseverance, which was the salt in our woman cake.

As a young woman, when life's challenges, brought heartache and doubt, you were always there to keep me grounded and together, like the eggs, shortening and liquid that bind the ingredients together.

When I left home, became a wife and started life on my own, new life experiences created the flavorings that began to fall into the mix. Life's ups and downs continued the process and stirred the batter well.

As a mother I began to truly take form, as the batter grew and transformed into cake, a cherished dessert. Time passes as the cake bakes, then cools and prepares for the next step.

Becoming a grandmother is certainly the icing on the cake. But then you already knew that, for my children were blessed to realize the value of family love and support through you.

Life has shaped me into the woman I am, but the essential ingredients you blessed me with are what give the form substance. These are the things that make the cake taste good. I am so thankful that God chose you to bake my Blue Ribbon cake.

www.ingramcontent.com/pod-product-compliance
Lightning Source LLC
LaVergne TN
LVHW061552070526
838199LV00077B/7021